A SCRIPTURAL EXAMINATION OF THE INSTITUTION OF SLAVERY IN THE UNITED STATES

With Its Objects and Purposes

by
Howell Cobb

THE CONFEDERATE
REPRINT COMPANY
☆   ☆   ☆   ☆
WWW.CONFEDERATEREPRINT.COM

A Scriptural Examination of the Institution
of Slavery in the United States
by Howell Cobb

Originally Published in 1856
by Howell Cobb
Georgia

Reprint Edition © 2014
The Confederate Reprint Company
Post Office Box 2027
Toccoa, Georgia 30577
www.confederatereprint.com

Cover and Interior by
Magnolia Graphic Design
www.magnoliagraphicdesign.com

ISBN-13: 978-0692301029
ISBN-10: 069230102X

PREFACE

☆   ☆   ☆   ☆

The Particular Object of This Work

We have not undertaken to write the general history of slavery, nor the history of slavery in the United States; the extent of our undertaking is, to show the purposes for which African slavery was instituted, in so far as the United States stand connected with it. There are two propositions of essential importance, and which never must be lost sight of, in the investigation of this subject, to wit:

1. *African slavery is a punishment, inflicted upon the enslaved, for their wickedness.* The proper understanding of this proposition requires that we should keep steadily before the mind the fact, that nations, communities, peoples, may and do sin against God, as well as individuals; and nations, communities, peoples, are punishable and punished, as well as individuals. The only difference is this: individuals may escape punishment; they often do, in this world: their punishment may be postponed to the day of judgment; but nations, communities, peoples, must be punished in this world, for they cannot, as such, be brought into the judgment of the great day.

2. *Slavery, as it exists in the United States, is the Providentially-arranged means whereby Africa is to be lifted from her deep degradation, to a state of civil and religious liberty.*

3

It must not be supposed, that in the performance of this task we desire to present an apology for slavery, or to conciliate favor for it; we have no such intention or object in view. An institution of Divine appointment does not need the aid of human writers, further than an explanation of its meaning.

Why should any one be astonished at slavery? This is not the only time that it has been employed as a means of working out great purposes. God's chosen and peculiar people; they who first composed the Church; they to whom the oracles of salvation were delivered; they of whom the prophets were; they from whom the Redeemer of the world sprang, were enslaved in as hard, perhaps in much harder bondage, than has ever been experienced by Africans in the United States – a bondage from which they were delivered only after a series of the most astonishing displays of the Divine displeasure, inflicted upon their oppressors for their obstinacy in refusing "to let the people go."

Nor was Egyptian bondage the only bondage they experienced, for their history shows that there were repeated instances of captivity, during which they were subject to the most degrading and humiliating slavery. And their history further shows, that these instances of captivity were inflicted as punishments upon them for their unfaithfulness to God, in disobeying His commands.

Nor was this mode of punishment confined to the Hebrews; for, the sacred record shows, that it was frequently threatened and inflicted upon other nations. Indeed, we may say, slavery has ever been a common mode of divine punishment inflicted upon nations.

The Bible Our Authority

We have been directed, in the execution of the more important portions of our undertaking, by the Bible; that is our sole authority for many things which we have written in this volume. Men may and will question, controvert, and discuss, everything of human origin, and agree or disagree with their authors, as they think proper; but when the Bible speaks there is an end to controversy and discussion: our duty then becomes very simple; it is – to be silent – to listen – to understand – to obey: for this authority no man may question or disregard.

Mutation is stamped upon everything in nature, and everything of human origin. There is nothing immutable in this world, but one thing; that is the Bible – it never changes: amidst the endless and unceasing change occurring, the Bible continues unchangeable. Like the sun, the great center of the solar system, the Bible maintains one position, reducing to order and quiet the confusion of the moral universe. Our adoration is demanded, as we see the wonderful Book of God adapting its lessons of instruction to each passing event, as if they had been prepared exclusively for that. Let changes occur as they may – let the aspect of society be what it will – let the conduct of individuals assume never so strange and uncommon a character, the Bible meets all with a distinctness and particularity neither to be mistaken or misunderstood – commanding what ought to be done, and forbidding what ought not to be done, in each particular case; at the same time leaving man to act as he will: hence, man's responsibility. In all this we see reflected forth the divinity of the Bible.

The Bible is *one word*; it teaches that the Godhead is composed of three persons; namely, the Father, the Son, and the Holy Ghost; hence the Bible consists of three parts; or more properly, of three revelations, or dispensations; that is to say, 1. The revelation of the Father: under this dispensation the *precepts* of religion were made known, and most of the prophecies delivered. 2. The revelation of the Son: under this dispensation, the precepts revealed under the dispensation of the Father were *amplified*, the prophecies fulfilled, and the stringency of many rules relaxed. 3. The revelation of the Holy Ghost: under this dispensation, the precepts and prophecies revealed under the dispensation of the Father, and amplified and fulfilled under the dispensation of the Son, were *spiritualized*. Each of these dispensations had its ministry and ordinances, or form of worship, to wit: under the dispensation of the Father, *priests* were the ministers; at the head of this ministry was the high-priest. Under the dispensation of the Son, *apostles* were the ministers; at the head of this ministry was our Lord Jesus Christ. Under the dispensation of the Holy Ghost, *preachers* are the ministers; at the head of this ministry stands St. Paul. So with the ordinances under the dispensation of the Father, circumcision and the passover were instituted in the Church. Under the dispensation of the Son, baptism was observed in connection with circumcision. After the resurrection of our Lord, He commanded that circumcision should be dropped; or rather, that baptism alone should be continued: under this dispensation, too, the passover was changed into the sacrament of the Lord's Supper; in which manner these ordinances are now observed in the Church. These three parts form one grand and glorious scheme of salvation.

 Slavery was established in the Church under the first dispensation, or the dispensation of the Father, and recognized and regulated under all the dispensations.

Divine Providence

Providence may be defined to be, God's care manifested in every circumstance and event, over and above all human sagacity and prudence. It extends to the minutest particulars and objects: "Are not two sparrows sold for a farthing? and one of them shall not fall on the ground without your Father. But the very hairs of your head are all numbered. Fear ye not therefore, ye are of more value than many sparrows." Very many providential occurrences are profoundly mysterious, the explanations of which must be referred to the day of judgment, when their propriety will be made manifest. Providence is a subject requiring the profoundest *yes !* study: it neither forces human conduct, nor prevents it.

The Providence of God is taught in the following Scripture: "Except the Lord build the house, they labor in vain that build it: except the Lord keep the city, the watchman waketh but in vain." The obvious meaning here, is that, however prudent and skilful we may be in the affairs of life, unless God's blessing be upon our efforts, we cannot succeed; whenever, therefore, success attends our efforts, we are to remember that we are indebted to Providence for it.

Providence is not religion, nor is it necessarily connected with religion; for, "He maketh His sun to rise on the evil and on the good, and sendeth rain on the just and on the unjust."

Although the action of Providence is to be observed in connection with every event, and all circumstances, yet every man may observe in his own case some occurrence purely Providential; that is to say, some occurrence in which God's care, producing him good, or preserving him from harm, without any agency on his part, distinctly manifests itself.

The manifestations of Providence, as connected with African slavery, are distinctly seen, in all its variations and in every particular. "O the depth of the riches, both of the wisdom and knowledge of God! How unsearchable are His judgments, and His ways past finding out!"

They who have been attentive to the workings of Providence, have observed, that all great enterprises have their attendant sacrifices. The promised land was not possessed by the descendants of Abraham, but after overcoming in war the fiercest struggles of the Canaanites – struggles in which the Israelites lost thousands of their people. The long, fierce and sanguinary wars with the natives and others, which the settlers of the United States were compelled to maintain – wars, in which many thousands of them were slain, attest the truth of the great fact here stated. Africa is not to be exempt from the common lot – she must pay for the great boon to be secured: and it will be seen upon consideration, that the sacrifices made by Africa, in view of the good to be realized, are perhaps much less than any other nation has been required to make.

Let the reader contemplate well the condition of Africa; let him understand fully all the particulars that make up that condition: every trace of an idea of God, correctly entertained, lost, so that the prophet says of her, "There is no God;" every social and civil virtue extinct, and every vice of which the mind can conceive, adopted and practiced, and then measure the degradation of Africa, if he can. Now, the Gospel is to redeem Africa from all this – is it a large price that Africa pays for this incalculable good? Is it not a price immeasurably below the good to be realized? Who does not see that Africa is to be the beneficiary of the arrangement?

The idea that African slavery in the United States was to be beneficial to the slaves, was entertained in Georgia over one hundred years ago, and before that kind of slavery existed in the colony. Then Mr. James Habersham wrote: "I once thought it was unlawful to keep Negro slaves, but I am now induced to think that God may have a higher end in permitting them to be brought to this Christian country, than merely to support their masters. Many of the poor slaves in America have already been made freemen of the heavenly Jersualem; and, possibly, a time may come when many thousands may embrace the Gospel, and thereby be brought into the glorious liberty of the children of God." Mr. Habersham was not a prophet, but he was among the distinguished statesmen of his day. He was a humane master, and a sagacious and consistent Christian.

Slavery of the Church

The system of slavery established in the Church, protects the life of the slave against the cruelty or wantonness of the master. The law says: "And if a man smite his servant or his maid with a rod, and he die under his hand, he shall be surely punished: notwithstanding, if he continue a day or two, he shall not be punished, for he is his money." The punishment to be inflicted, in case the slave died under his master's hand, was death. The law continues: "At the hand of every man's brother will I require the life of man. Whoso sheddeth man's blood, by man shall his blood be shed; for in the image of God made He man." It is easy to see, therefore, that every system of slavery which does not forbid the master taking the life of a slave, or using cruelty towards him, and which does not properly punish the crime when committed, is an abuse of the Divine establishment. Such were the systems of the

Roman and Grecian States; such has ever been the African system; and such, perhaps, were the English and French systems while they existed. The fact that the English system of African slavery did not protect the life of the slave was one of the most potent reasons brought forward by English abolitionists while urging emancipation.

We assert, and we shall prove, that the system of slavery in the United States, in every feature and in every particular of every feature, is essentially the same as the system authorized by the Bible, and introduced into the church at the time of its organization, and continued to the present day. The Bible does not employ the term slave, but the more significant term servant. Servant is the correct term with us; it should be used instead of the harsher term slave, which is neither expressive nor true. In this work, however, we have used the term slave, simply for convenience sake, and in conformity to custom.

Master

Webster defines this term thus: "A man who rules, governs, or directs either men or business. A man who owns slaves is their master; he who has servants is their master; he who has apprentices is their master, as he has the government and direction of them." There are many very important obligations imposed upon masters, some by the municipal law, all by the Bible. These obligations form the sum of a master's responsibility. The municipal law and the Bible, therefore, are the sources from which a master is to learn his duty to his slaves.

Servant

The term slave occurs but seldom in the Bible, perhaps not more than twice, and in no place in the sense in which it is generally used by us. The terms used which denote slavery, are servant, bondman, bondwoman, maid, handmaid, &c. As there are other servants besides slaves frequently spoken of, we must refer to the circumstances of each particular case, for the purpose of ascertaining the condition that is meant. Martindale says: "The word [servant] generally signifies a slave. The Hebrews had two sorts of servants or slaves." – See Lev. xxv. 44, 45.

Emancipation of Slaves

England, France, and all the States of the American Union, possessed Negro slaves at one time. England, France, and the Northern States have emancipated their slaves. They were right in so doing, for they never looked beyond pecuniary advantage in possessing them. They made no arrangements for their slaves' moral and religious training, such things were never thought of; no record testifies in their favor in this respect; no proofs can be furnished to support such a pretension. By repudiating slavery, England, France and the Northern States, *declined participating in the objects, present and ultimate, of the institution. They withdrew from this great Providential enterprise.*

In favor of English effort in the direction contemplated, we may be pointed to Sierra Leone. The feeble efforts made there do not even make a qualification of our assertion necessary. Let us see. During the war of the Revolution, many American slaves were seduced to the British army, then in the country. Some of them were conveyed to England and some to Nova Scotia. Those that went to England, lounging about London, in a most filthy and miserable condition, excited the sympathy of some benevolent individuals. These persons made efforts, which resulted in the colonization of the Negroes in Africa. This occurred more than seventy years ago. That during this long period some good has been done, we with pleasure acknowledge; but not the amount of good that ought to have been done, by a great deal. Compare the good done by the colonization of Sierra Leone, with that done by the colonization of Liberia, and it will be seen that the statement we have made above needs no qualification.

Liberia was colonized less than forty years ago (a little over half the time that Sierra Leone has been colonized), and during the period that has intervened has passed through the incipient stages of government to a republic, in which every element of civil, intellectual, moral and religious improvement abounds. Her influence extends far into the interior, over many tribes and nations. She has accomplished more during the brief period of her existence to suppress the slave-trade, than the combined efforts of all civilized nations ever accomplished, or were likely to accomplish.

Abolitionists

There are persons in the Northern section of the Union, who, having no proper conceptions of the institution of slavery, seek to destroy it: these persons are denominated abolitionists. Amongst these persons there exists many shades of difference: 1. The freesoiler – this character, who will not admit that he is an abolitionist in the proper sense of the term, professes that he does not wish to disturb slavery where it exists, but opposes the enlargement of its area. 2. The conditional emancipationist – he professes that he would be satisfied if the South would pass acts of emancipation, although such acts might extend through many years. 3. The unconditional emancipationist – he demands that acts of emancipation should be passed, abolishing the institution of slavery forthwith. 4. The amalgamationist – he demands that slavery should be abolished immediately – that there should be a division of property with the emancipated slaves and an amalgamation with the whites. It is a matter of perfect indifference to us, to which of these phases individuals may be attached; for we care not whether, in their folly, they be mild or rabid.

Abolitionism is not a political question; *it is a religious delusion*; hence, the political adjustments of the question have, in the end, all failed to accomplish their object. These adjustments have only resulted in causing abolitionism to assume some new aspect; to turn its mischievous tendencies in some new direction. The profound regard which every American citizen should feel and manifest for the Constitution, the priceless value of the union of the States, and the clearest, most comprehensive and conclusive arguments of anti-abolitionists, have lost their force, when addressed to abolitionists.

 This delusion may be distinctly traced to its source – *it sprang from misguided religious teachers;* by them it has been, and is now being, taught to the people. It is a fact upon which we dwell with pleasure, that many teachers of religion in the Northern States, have never been under the influence of this delusion. These cannot agree to prostitute their high and holy vocation to such unworthy purposes. Designing newspaper editors, both secular and religious, fond of filthy lucre (particularly in the form of blackmail), have contributed largely to inflame the minds of the uninformed; thereby degrading the liberty of the press, and robbing it of its influence for good. Corrupt politicians, too, the basest of all, have made this delusion subservient to their schemes of ambition. Honest and honorable politicians, they who would not stoop to expedients so low, have been turned out of office and sent into private life. These are some of the workings of abolitionism.

Wow !! There is nothing more disgusting than abolitionism – nothing, we consider, more wicked and mischievous; yet we confess that we do not fear it. Many very considerate persons suppose that it will ultimately destroy the Union; in this opinion we do not participate: that it would do that act if it could, we readily allow – we firmly believe; but it has not vitality enough to accomplish that result, we conceive. We cannot, at present, be induced to believe that God, whose hand is so signally seen in every step of our progress, will allow deluded men, no matter what their numbers may be, or how intemperate their zeal, to consummate such great wickedness. The issue, Union or Abolitionism, may be presented to the American people; it will be, if abolitionists can do it. Should that issue be presented, the anti-abolitionists of the North (for there are many Union-loving people there, who are to be found in all the walks of life), will not require the aid of the South in putting down this bad spirit; they will perform that very agreeable duty for themselves. Whether abolitionism is to be feared or not, however, the South must not abate one iota of its vigilance against it.

It is an established fact, that the mind may become unsettled by the long and abstract consideration of any subject upon which it may concentrate its energies. In other words, the mind may become insane upon one subject, while upon all other subjects it remains rational. An author says: "Such partial derangement is the most singular feature of the human character: one can easily imagine that the whole mind should become disordered and prostrated; but that one part should be deranged, while the rest retains its wonted vigor; that a man should be capable to create a perfect phantom of the imagination, and then to reason and act upon it as though it were a reality, is most unaccountable; and yet such instances have frequently occurred." Our author goes on to state a case: "One Wood, indicted Dr. Monro, in Westminster, for keeping him as a prisoner in a mad-house, when he was sane. He underwent the most severe examination by the defendant's counsel, without exposing his complaint; but a physician suggested to Lord Mansfield to ask him what was become of the princess with whom he had corresponded in cherry-juice; he showed in a moment what he was. He answered, that there was nothing at all in that, because having been (as everybody knew) imprisoned in a high tower, and being debarred the use of ink, he had no other means of correspondence but by writing his letters in cherry-juice, and throwing them into the river which surrounded the tower, where the princess received them in a boat: on this Dr. Monro was acquitted." This affords the best apology for abolitionists that can be made for them.

This degree of madness is by no means incurable: for its cure, the people of the South possess an unfailing remedy, which has been applied to many patients, and which will never fail to be applied, whenever it becomes necessary. As to the efficacy of this remedy, many who have been cured, live to testify their gratitude, and to bless their benefactors.

The efforts of abolitionists have made no impression whatever on the institution of slavery in the United States, although long continued and vigorously pressed. Individual slave-owners have been injured, but the institution remains unharmed; it is as vigorous, firm, and flourishing, to-day, as it has ever been since its foundation, and so is likely to continue.

Amongst the most successful schemes of mischief brought forth by abolitionists, may be reckoned what is familiarly called the Under-Ground Railroad: by this means, many owners have been deprived of their property by persons esteeming themselves, and being esteemed by their associates, pious. How strong must be the delusion, when professing Christians conceive that there is no sin in stealing! There have been many punished in various ways, no doubt, who have been engaged in this systematized mode of villany. A recent case has fallen under our notice: one McCormick, a member of the Cumberland Presbyterian Synod of Indiana, was suspended from the ministry (a very inadequate punishment) for his connection with it. This foolish man was not even a successful rogue; he betrayed himself by boasting of his performances.

Sometimes works of fiction (we had a specimen of this kind of erudition recently) make their appearance: these purport to be intended to inflame the popular mind, by relating cases of hardship endured by slaves, and thereby to hasten the destruction of the institution. It is suspected, however, that the authoress of the work alluded to (with true Yankee shrewdness), had a more attentive eye in the direction of the money to be realized from the sale of her work, than to the success of the principles she advocated in it.

Sometimes indiscreet individuals of this character propagate their sentiments on Southern soil; nothing can be more hazardous – *this cannot, will not, be allowed.* In not a few cases of this kind, the offender has received summarily such chastisement as would deter him from a like undertaking for the future, and which would be an effectual admonition to all others in like manner disposed to offend.

A few foreigners, of sufficient notoriety to claim our attention, in the exuberance of their benevolence, and with a philanthropy that unfortunately overlooks the squalidity of their own country and neighborhoods, have visited the United States occasionally for the purpose of our enlightenment on the subject of slavery. Among the most notorious of these, one George Thompson is, perhaps, the most conspicuous. This man, possessing some powers of declamation, and much intemperate zeal, made his appearance here some years ago. He was the employee of some old Scotch ladies, not much wiser than himself, who picked him out of some sewer in the purlieus of Glasgow, or some other filthy place. It is matter of some surprise that the efforts of this abolition agent were not extended to those they were intended to benefit! He confined his labors to the Northern section of the Union, and to a very small portion of the people there, members of anti-slavery associations. It is, perhaps, matter of regret that Thompson did not extend his visits into the South, for it is probable had he done so, in the report he made to his employers, upon his return to his own country, he would have had the pleasure of adding some *tangible* proofs of his *personal* reception.

Of another foreigner (Hon. Miss Murray, a lady lately attached to the Court of Queen Victoria), it affords us much pleasure to speak in different language. This lady visited the South with all the prejudices of early education, and long-cherished convictions against us. These prejudices were highly inflamed by imagined and reported cases of hardship, said to be common among slave-holders. She came, she heard, she saw for herself, and the truth worked an entire revolution in her opinions and feelings. It is matter of deep regret that Miss Murray's determination to publish her knowledge of slavery in the United States, if it did not cause the alienation of her friend, nevertheless caused the cessation of the patronage of that friend. This is not only matter of regret to us, it is matter of surprise also. Her Majesty may have suffered herself to be persuaded that something of State-policy was involved in the course she was advised to pursue towards Miss Murray's book. However this may be, we regret the course pursued, because we assert that, personally, no sovereign now occupying a throne, is wont to be more highly regarded by the people of the United States than is her Britannic Majesty.

It is supposed by some that we have abolitionists residing

amongst us, who are engaged in various lucrative employments; the supposition is well founded. Persons thus situated will best consult their safety by concealing their opinions. This caution, however, may be unnecessary, as those to whom it refers understand as well as we do the prudent line of conduct.

It is also proper to remark, that many persons located amongst us, who were formerly abolitionists – made so by the false teachings to which they were confined – have, since they became acquainted with the practical operations of the institution of slavery, and its objects, thoroughly changed their opinions, and are now as trustworthy on the subject, as if they had never been imposed upon.

It is impossible to conceive the amount of mischief abolitionism has done, and is seeking to do. Its broad slime-trace is to be seen in every direction. It invades the sanctuary of law, and strikes the balance from the hand of justice; it tramples upon the Constitution; it repudiates the Bible; it has rended asunder the Church of the living God; it sports with everything holy and sacred; it commits murder; it has progressed far in destroying the comity between the States; it now menaces the integrity of the Union itself! This, however, we trust, is as far as it will be allowed, by the patriotism of the people, to progress. A spirit so emphatically "devilish," demands that every patriot in the land should make haste to put it down.

We address one word to abolitionists not so far gone in their madness as to be incapable of appreciating what we say and mean: "And now I say unto you, Refrain from these men [slaveholders], and let them alone, for if this counsel, or this work [slavery], be of men [simply human], it will come to nought; but if it be of God [as we shall show it is], ye cannot overthrow it; lest, haply, ye [abolitionists] be found even to fight against God." We know that the foregoing quotation is from a source not much, if at all, respected by abolitionists; yet we think the advice it contains good, and that it ought to be observed. Whether it be followed or not, however, is matter of perfect indifference to us.

What an amusing spectacle abolitionism personified would

be! Were some skilful play-writer to employ his talents in this way, and produce a play, called *The Abolitionist*; consisting of as many parts as there are phases amongst abolitionists; in which brother Gardner, brother Seward (with a roll in his hand, marked "higher law"), brother Trumbull, brother Parker, brother Greeley (with a slouched hat on his head), brother Wilson, brother Smith, brother Beecher (with a Sharp's rifle on his shoulder), brother Garrison, and their brother Fred, *miserabile vulgus*; and those strong-minded women, aunt Harriet, sister Rev. Antoinette, sister Lucy (displaying a marriage protest), sister Abbe, and *their* sister the Black Swan (*et id genus omne*), should have conspicuous places; to conclude with the farce of *A Cured Abolitionist Returning From the South*; over all which his Satanic Majesty, who has the perfect right, should be seen, with grinning approbation, to preside; it is probable he would produce as ludicrous an exhibition as was ever presented to the gaze of an admiring audience.

Emancipating Slaves

True

There is no power, divine or human, that requires an owner to emancipate his slave. If that be done, it must be a voluntary act, by all the parties concerned – voluntary on the part of the owner, in offering emancipation, and voluntary on the part of the slave, in accepting it. Supposing an owner to be inclined to emancipate his slave, no one has any right to object, no one does object; for the owner has as perfect a right to dispose of his slave property, as he has to dispose of any other species of property he may possess.

The troubles and responsibilities of an owner are not few or small, as everyone well knows. In view of these considerations, owners are sometimes induced to emancipate their slaves, by sending them all, old, middle-aged, and young, to Africa; nothing, we conceive, is of greater impropriety. In such case the owner gets rid of the inconveniences alluded to, but the slave's condition is much worse than it could have been if he had remained with his owner. The fever peculiar to Africa, called the acclimating fever, which every emigrant must pass through, destroys, as the bills of mortality show, a great many of the very young and the very old; indeed, so many of these die, that it may be truly said they go there but to be buried. Besides, emigrants of this description embarrass those upon whom they are dependent, and are useless, if not expensive, to the government. These things should be well considered by every owner disposed to emancipate his slaves.

The propriety of emancipating a slave, in view of his transportation to Africa, requires: 1. That the slave be particularly instructed with regard to all the difficulties and dangers he will have to meet in his new situation. 2. That he be in good health, and of a sound constitution. 3. That he be of good moral character. 4. That he be industrious and provident. 5. That he be willing to go. These particulars being ascertained, and the slave being furnished by his owner with such things as will be necessary for his convenience for the first year of his residence in Africa, and the payment of his passage thither, let him go.

The conveying emancipated slaves to Africa by the Colonization Society, is an incidental undertaking. That society was organized, and still continues to exist, for the exclusive purpose of transporting the free persons of color in the United States to Africa. The society, therefore, should not be expected to divert its means from the direct to an incidental object; indeed, in many instances, the intentions of owners have been defeated, from the fact that the society has been unable to sustain the expenses of the slaves they proposed to emancipate.

Mahometanism

This system of religion, if it be allowable to dignify it with such a title, may properly be divided into two parts, namely: creed and practice. The creed embraces some leading truths, improperly conceived, and, therefore, badly taught, and many absurdities – perhaps we would be more correct in calling them profanities. The creed is reduced to a very simple form, thus: "God is God, and Mahomet is His prophet." This must be believed.

The practice consists of four general parts, thus: 1. Prayer. 2. Alms, of which there are two kinds, namely: legal and voluntary. 3. Fasting – this Mahometans call "the gate of religion." 4. The pilgrimage to Mecca; they say a Moslem had as well die a Jew or a Christian, in either of which cases there is no chance for heaven, as to die without having performed this pilgrimage.

This religion is now, as it has been from the first, propagated by force – compulsion is the instrument it employs to make converts. This is the religion of Northern, from whence it has been carried far into Central, but it has not yet reached Southern Africa. There, until Christian missionaries made their appearance, there was no God taught in any form!

The Christianizing of Africa involves the fact, that on that field Christianity and Mahometanism are to engage in their contests, to fight their battles. There the crescent and the cross are to meet face to face. Already the warrior hosts of Christianity are buckling on their armor. In the name of the living God they go forth, and in the name of the living God they shall triumph. The crescent shall bow to the cross. When we survey the whole ground, we see what a mighty work Christianity has to perform in Africa!

Exodus of Slavery

Whether slavery is a temporary or permanent institution, has been deemed an important inquiry. The thorough investigation of this question does not properly fall within the range of our undertaking; for we are not interested in hypothetical but historical facts. All that we shall do here, therefore, will be to exhibit the expressed opinions of some men of distinguished abilities on the subject, and submit some general remarks for the consideration of the reader.

Mr. Clay, who thinks the institution temporary, says: "I believe, and I have as much confidence in the belief as I have in my own existence, that the day will come, distant, very far distant, perhaps, from the present time, but that the day will come, *when, by voluntary emancipation, and by acts of individuals, and of the States themselves, without any usurpation of power on the part of the general government, there will be an end of slavery.* Slavery may find its termination in different modes. It may by law; it may by the sword; it may by the operation of natural causes, to which I look for its ultimate extinction. As to the sword, nobody, I trust, would think of the employment of that to put an end to slavery.

"But I may be asked, What is meant by the operation of natural causes? I mean this: upon one occasion, some twenty years ago, I went more at large than I feel now at liberty to do, into this subject. I went into the *modus operandi* of these natural causes, by which, in a long time, I am of opinion there will be an extinction of slavery. There will be an extinction of slavery whenever the density of the population in the United States shall be so great that free labor can be procured by those who want the command of labor at a cheaper rate, and under less onerous conditions, than slave labor can be commanded. Although I cannot fix the time when this will occur, I can state the conditions and circumstances under which. When it does occur, there will be *a voluntary manumission of slaves*. It is not to be by any enforced usurpation or legal action of the general, or any other government at all, but by the voluntary consent of the States, and individuals of the States, which are alone interested in the subject of slavery, and which have exclusively the right to determine when and how it shall cease to exist. Whenever, then, you can show to me, and that time will come, that our population shall be three or four times as great as it is, and that time will not be a very long time – when we measure time not by the duration of individuals or particular lives of persons, but by the period of national existence – whenever the time comes, as it will come, that our population shall be three or four times as great as at present; that the prices of labor, the wages of manual labor, shall be so reduced that it will be too burdensome on the part of the owners of slaves to raise them for the sake of the labor they perform; whenever it becomes the interest of the slave States and the slave-holders to resort to another kind of labor than that which is furnished by slaves; whenever that e-

poch comes, there will be a termination of slavery. Now, gentle-
men, I am not about, as I said before, to specify the time when this
is going to happen – I cannot do it – but I would repress, if I
could, the impatience of those who are unwilling to wait the slow
operation of the means and instrumentalities which God and nature furnish in order to accomplish the great purposes of His wisdom. I would ask them to repress their impatience; to have more
dependence upon the wisdom and providence of God than upon
their own limited passions and circumscribed reason. What, in a
national point of view, is a century to a nation? Nothing. It took
two centuries and more to bring from the shores of Africa her
sons, now existing in a state of slavery in the United States. It may
take two centuries, more or less, to transport their descendants, to
such an extent as no longer to create any solicitude or anxiety
about the few that may linger and remain behind. It may take some
two centuries to carry them back; and what, I repeat again, is this
in the great workings of national existence, and the administration
of the affairs of this world, by the Providence that controls, directs, and governs them?"

Mr. Toombs says: "His condition [the African slave] is not
permanent among us, and we may find his exodus in the unvarying
laws of population. Under the conditions of labor in England, and
the continent of Europe, slavery could not exist here, or anywhere
else. The moment wages descend to a point barely sufficient to
support the laborer and his family, capital cannot afford to own
labor, and slavery instantly ceases. Slavery ceased in England in
obedience to this law, and not from any regard to liberty or humanity. The increase of population will produce the same result in
this country; and American slavery, like that of England, will find
its euthanasy in the general prostration of all labor."

The opinions we have presented above are decidedly in
favor of the institution being a temporary one. They are based
upon an assumed state of facts, which lie far in the future – a state
of facts warranted by no present indications. We do not intend to
question the soundness of these opinions; we do not intend to say
that they never will be realized; but we do intend to say, that noth-

ing connected with the practical operations of the institution points that way. We do not see "the beginning of the end." These opinions may, they may not, be correct. However that may be, they have no immediate bearing upon the institution. Being, therefore, of no present interest, these opinions (as their authors intended they should not) do not interfere in the slightest degree with the institution. *We who are connected with the institution at this day, are to regard it as permanent – perpetual.*

But, assuming that the institution is a temporary and not a permanent one, it is easy to see that society, in all its ramifications, will have to undergo a complete revolution, before it is abolished. This state of things, in which abolitionists will have no agency whatever, will be brought about by Providence in gradual movements, which, causing no detriment to any, will receive the hearty approval and cooperation of all.

Perry, Houston County, Ga.,
August, 1856.

CHAPTER ONE
Institution of Slavery

☆   ☆   ☆   ☆

Section 1

Noah's Posterity. – "And the sons of Noah, that went forth of the ark, were Shem, and Ham, and Japheth: and Ham is the father of Canaan: these are the three sons of Noah; and of them was the whole earth overspread."

Noah attained the age of nine hundred and fifty years; this period is divided thus; six hundred years before the deluge and three hundred and fifty years after that event. This makes the age of Noah the second highest on record, that of Methuselah being the first, he having lived nine hundred and sixty-nine years.

"And of them was the whole earth overspread." – Noah died Anno Mundi 2006, as is generally agreed. Previously to his death, he divided the earth among his three sons. Asia was assigned to Shem, Europe to Japheth, and Africa to Ham.

Prophecy concerning Slavery. – "And Noah began to be an husbandman, and he planted a vineyard: and he drank of the wine and was drunken; and he was uncovered within his tent. And Ham, the father of Canaan, saw the nakedness of his father, and told his brethren without.

"And Shem and Japheth took a garment, and laid it upon their shoulders, and went backward, and covered the nakedness of their father; and their faces were backward, and they saw not their father's nakedness.

"And Noah awoke from his wine, and knew what his younger son had done unto him. And he said. Cursed be Canaan; a servant of servants shall he be unto his brethren. And he said, Blessed be the Lord God of Shem, and Canaan shall be his servant. God shall enlarge Japheth, and he shall dwell in the tents of Shem, and Canaan shall be his servant."

How peculiarly emphatic is this language, "a servant of servants;" that is, the most degraded kind of servant – *a slave.* Here we have the establishment of the relation of master and servant; that is to say, slavery. This prophecy was delivered A. M. 1657, which must be regarded as the period of the establishment of slavery: its practical developments will appear as we progress.

But why was slavery established? We answer, as a punishment for sin. Upon whom was this particular punishment to be inflicted? We answer, upon Ham's posterity; for, however reprehensible we may regard the conduct of Ham towards his father to have been, we are not to suppose that that conduct was the cause of the curse pronounced upon his son Canaan; for had Ham's conduct been the cause of the curse, the curse would have been pronounced upon him and not upon his son. Ham's conduct was but the occasion that brought forth the announcement of events then far in the future, and which have been, and still are being, developed.

The text does not warrant the conclusion that Canaan participated in the mirth or contempt which the discovery of Noah's condition occasioned; the assertion that such was the fact is altogether gratuitous; it is unsupported by authority; it cannot be proved; it is not inferable. *Canaan's name is mentioned to denote Ham's posterity;* it is for that purpose alone that it is used in the prophecy. The whole prophecy must be taken together – Shem and Japheth had shown a virtuous regard for their father; that virtue manifested itself in their posterity – *it was that virtue that was blessed.* On the contrary, Ham's conduct was vicious; (vice in his posterity has ever been their most marked characteristic) – *it was that viciousness that was cursed,* and which has been punished in so peculiar a manner.

We are aware that we have assumed advanced ground in the above statement. The extent to which opinion has gone, on the subject of slavery, is at most, that it was but permitted, not ordained. That it was ordained by divine authority, and announced in the prophecy of Noah, is what we assert. This assertion we prove by two considerations: 1. The language of the prophecy is the language of *command*, not of *permission*. 2. By the fulfilment of the prophecy, which will be seen in the facts which compose the subsequent portions of this volume.

The view that we here submit may not be acceptable to all; it would be strange if it were so; but let no one reject it by saying, "I don't believe it." " I don't believe it," is the language of either ignorance or prejudice; sometimes of both. Let those who deny the correctness of our interpretation of the prophecy produce the proof and the argument which will show its incorrectness. Truth being our object, to proof and argument we will most cheerfully submit.

Section 2

Shem's Posterity. – Shem had five sons, namely, Elam, Asshur, Arphaxad, Lud and Aram. "Elam settled in Persia, where he became the father of that mighty nation. The descendants of Asshur, peopled Assyria. Arphaxad settled in Chaldea. To the family of Lud is generally assigned Lydia. Aram is believed to have settled in Mesopotamia and Syria."

Japheth's Posterity. – The Bible does not furnish any account of the life and death of Japheth; but that his sons, namely, Gomer, Magog, Madia, Javan, Jubal, Meshech, and Tiras, became the heads of nations, is generally believed. "Gomer," says Josephus, "was the father of the Gomerites, or Celts; that is, of all the nations that inhabited the northern parts of Europe, under the names of Gauls, Cimbrians, Goths, &c., and who also migrated into Spain, where they were called Celtiberians. From Magog, Meshech, and Jubal, proceeded the Scythians, Sarmatians, and Tartars. From Madia, Javan, and Tiras, the Medes, Ionians, Greeks and Thracians."

Ham's Posterity. – Ham had four sons, namely. Cush, Mizraim, Phut, and Canaan. "The sons of Cush, Seba, and Havilah, and Sabtah, and Raamah, and Sabtechah: and the sons of Raamah, Sheba and Dedan. And Cush begat Nimrod: he began to be a mighty one in the earth. He was a mighty hunter before the Lord: wherefore, it is said, Even as Nimrod, the mighty hunter before the Lord. And the beginning of his kingdom was Babel, and Erech, and Accad, and Calneh, in the land of Shinar. Out of that land went forth Asshur, and builded Nineveh, and the city Rehoboth, and Calah, and Resen, between Nineveh and Calah: the same is a great city."

As we are more interested in the posterity of Cush, than in that of the other sons of Ham, to wit, Mizraim, Phut, and Canaan, we shall first notice the latter. This course will enable us to keep our attention fixed uninterruptedly upon that people from whom came the slaves of the United States; in whose history, as well as it can be traced, we cannot but feel the liveliest interest.

Mizraim. – This son of Ham was the progenitor of the Egyptians, who are frequently called by his name: the word is also used as the name of the country. Mizraim has three different significations: 1. The land of Egypt. 2. Him who first peopled Egypt. 3. The inhabitants of Egypt.

Egypt is divided into two parts by the river Nile, which runs from north to south; hence, Lower and Upper Egypt. The capital of this country, Cairo, and even the country itself, is by the Arabians called Mezer: the natives call it Chemi, that is to say, the land of Ham: so it is sometimes called by the Hebrews. The Mizraimites settled that part of the land of Canaan known as Philistia, or Palestine: they have, long ago, been lost, as a distinct people.

Phut. – It is agreed that this son of Ham peopled a colony in Lower Egypt, inclining towards Lybia. His descendants, therefore, are generally reckoned among the Egyptians, and not as a distinct people. This branch of the Ham family, like that of Mizraim, has long ago disappeared.

Canaan. – "And Canaan begat Sidon, his first-born, and Heth, and the Jebusite, and the Emorite, and the Girgasite, and the Hivite, and the Arkite, and the Sinite, and the Arvadite, and the Zemarite and the Hamathite: and afterwards were the families of the Canaanites spread abroad. And the border of the Canaanites was from Sidon, as thou comest to Gerar, unto Gaza: as thou goest unto Sodom, and Gomorrah, and Admah, and Zeboim, even unto Lasha."

Canaan had, besides Sidon his first-born, ten other sons, who were the heads of as many tribes, all dwelling in Palestine and Syria. All these being Canaanites, the country took the name of "Canaan." The country thus named is "a narrow slip, extending along the eastern coast of the Mediterranean, from which to the river Jordan, the utmost width does not exceed fifty miles. The Jordan was the eastern boundary of the land of Canaan, or Palestine, properly so called: which derived its name from the Philistines, or Palestines, originally inhabiting the coast." After the Israelites possessed the country, it was considerably enlarged by the subjugation of neighboring nations. "The territory of Tyre and Sidon was its ancient border, on the northwest; the range of the Libanus and Anti-Libanus, forms a natural boundary on the north and northeast; while in the south it is pressed upon by the Syrian and Arabian deserts. The kingdom of David and Solomon extended far beyond these narrow limits: in a northeasterly direction, it was bounded only by the river Euphrates, and included a considerable part of Syria."

Section 8

The Canaanites to be exterminated, not enslaved. – Moses was the conductor of the Israelites, during their wanderings in the wilderness, but he was not permitted to accompany them into the promised land; when, therefore, they were prepared to pass the Jordan, their faithful legislator assembled them for his last instructions, and said: "When the Lord thy God shall bring thee into the land whither thou goest to possess it, and hast cast out many nations before thee, the Hittites, and the Girgashites, and the Amorites, and the Canaanites, and the Perizzites, and the Hivites, and the Jebusites, seven nations greater and mightier than thou; and when the Lord thy God shall deliver them before thee; thou shalt smite them, and utterly destroy them: thou shalt make no covenant with them, nor show mercy unto them: neither shalt thou make marriages with them; thy daughter thou shalt not give unto his son, nor his daughter shalt thou take unto thy son: for they will turn away thy son from following me, that they may serve other gods; so will the anger of the Lord be kindled against you, and destroy thee suddenly.

"And thou shalt consume all the people which the Lord thy God shall deliver thee; thine eye shall have no pity upon them: neither shalt thou serve their gods; for that will be a snare unto thee.

"But if ye will not drive out the inhabitants of the land from before you, then it shall come to pass that those which ye let remain of them, shall be pricks in your eyes, and thorns in your sides, and shall vex you in the land wherein ye dwell. Moreover, it shall come to pass, that I shall do unto you, as I thought to do unto them."

That nothing connected with the purgation of the promised land, might be left uncertain, Moses gave instructions with regard to the places of worship of the Canaanites: "Ye shall utterly destroy all the places wherein the nations which ye shall possess, served their gods; upon the high mountains, and upon the hills, and under every green tree, and ye shall overthrow their altars, and break their pillars, and burn their groves with fire; and ye shall hew down the graven images of their gods, and destroy the names of them, out of that place."

Josephus, speaking of Moses' instructions, says: "When you have beaten your enemies in battle, slay those that have fought against you, but preserve the others alive, that they may pay you tribute, excepting the nation of the Canaanites, for, as to that people, you must entirely destroy them." Again: "Moses directed, that when they had got possession of the land of the Canaanites, and when they had destroyed the whole multitude of its inhabitants, as they ought to do, they should erect an altar," &c. From the directness of the instructions given, both as related to the peoples of Canaan and their places of worship, it is impossible to understand anything less than a total extermination of both; that nothing should be left, either of the one or the other, whereby the Israelites should be corrupted.

So particular was Moses on this occasion, that he guarded the Israelites from improper conclusions: he knew they might attribute the wonderful displays of God's power through them to their own righteousness. That they might not fall into this error, he said: "Speak not in thine heart, after that the Lord thy God hath cast them out from before thee, saying. For my righteousness the Lord hath brought me in to possess this land; but for the wickedness of these nations, the Lord doth drive them out from before thee. Nor for thy righteousness, or for the uprightness of thine heart, dost thou go to possess their land, but for the wickedness of these nations, the Lord thy God doth drive them out from before thee; and that He may perform the word which the Lord sware unto thy fathers, Abraham, Isaac and Jacob, understand, therefore, that the Lord thy God giveth thee not this good land to possess it for thy righteousness, for thou art a stiff-necked people."

Section 4

Manner of executing the command. – "And the Lord thy God will put out those nations before thee by little and little: thou mayest not consume them at once, lest the beast of the field increase upon thee. But the Lord thy God shall deliver them unto thee, and thou shalt destroy them with a mighty destruction, until they be destroyed."

Respecting the situation of the seven nations, against whom the Israelites were first to proceed, Calmet remarks: "Those called Canaanites chiefly inhabited what is called Phoenicia, the environs of Tyre and Sidon; the Hittites occupied the mountains southward of the promised land; the Hivites dwelt by Ebal and Gerezim, Sichem and Gibeon, towards the mountains of Hermon; the Perizzites were, probably, not a distinct nation or tribe, but rather villagers, scattered through the country in general; the Girgashites possesseth the country beyond the Jordan, towards the lake of Gennesareth; the Jebusites possessed Jerusalem, and the Amorites occupied the mountainous country in the vicinity of the western part of the Dead Sea, and also that part of the land of Moab which the Israelites conquered from Sihon and Og."

Joshua, upon whom was devolved the duty of conducting the Israelites into the promised land, commenced the subjugation of the country and the extermination of its peoples, by first besieging the city of Jericho. Just as the city was about to fall, Joshua said to the Israelites: "The city shall be accursed, even it and all that are therein, to the Lord: only Rahab, the harlot, shall live, she and all that are with her in the house, because she hid the messengers that we sent." When the city fell, they utterly destroyed all that were in it, "both man and woman, young and old, and ox and sheep and ass, with the edge of the sword."

From the ruin of Jericho the Israelites proceeded to Ai. God said to Joshua: "Thou shalt do to Ai and her king as thou didst unto Jericho and her king." Upon the taking of Ai, the Israelites "smote it with the edge of the sword. And so it was, that all that fell that day, both of men and women, were twelve thousand, even all the men of Ai."

The narrative of Joshua's progress is here interrupted by an interesting circumstance. The Gibeonites (alias Hivites) having learned the fate of Jericho and Ai, "Did work wilily, and went and made as if they had been ambassadors; and took old sacks upon their asses, and wine bottles, old and rent, and bound up; and old shoes and clouted upon their feet, and old garments upon them; and all the bread of their provision was dry and mouldy." Thus prepared, they appeared in the camp of the Israelites and said: "We be come from a far country; now, therefore, make a league with us." The usual course of proceeding, by "asking counsel of the mouth of the Lord," was not observed by the Israelites. This fact is the more astonishing, because the Israelites suspected imposition on the part of the Gibeonites. The Israelites not only "took of their victuals," but "the princes of the congregation sware unto them," Joshua asked them: "Who are ye and from whence come ye?" They replied, that their country was very distant; that they had heard of the delivery, by the Lord, of the Israelites from Egypt, and of what the Lord had done to the Amorites on the other side of Jordan; therefore, their elders and people had sent them to meet the Israelites and ask terms of peace. In confirmation of the truth of their being a distant people, they referred to their mouldy bread; to their rent and torn wine bottles, and to their tattered garments. Joshua made a league with them. It is proper here to remark, that the extent of the league was "to let them live" – that is, not to exterminate them.

At the end of three days, the Israelites discovered the imposition of the Gibeonites, who, instead of living in a distant country, were the "neighbors" of the Israelites. Joshua proceeded to their country. "Now their cities were Gibeon, and Chephirah, and Beeroth, and Kirjath-jearim. And the Israelites smote them not, because the princes of the congregation had sworn unto them by the Lord God of Israel." Joshua summoned them before him, and said unto them: "Wherefore have ye beguiled us, saying, We are very far from you, when ye dwell among us? Now, therefore, ye are cursed, and there shall none of you be free from being bondmen, and hewers of wood and drawers of water, for the house of my God. And they answered Joshua and said, Because it was certainly told thy servants, how that the Lord thy God commanded his servant Moses to give you all the land, *and to destroy all the inhabitants of the land from before you;* therefore, we were sore afraid of our lives because of you, and have done this thing. And now, behold, we are in thine hand; as it seemeth good and right unto thee to do unto us, do." Joshua, on this, confirmed what had previously been determined upon; that is, he spared their lives, "because of the oath," and settled their condition of "hewers of wood and drawers of water;" that is, he reduced them to slavery.

Here we see that the Gibeonites were reduced to slavery by Joshua, but we do not find anywhere his authority for that act; indeed, he was "beguiled" into it by the Gibeonites, "not having sought counsel at the mouth of the Lord." Joshua cannot be justified on the ground of Noah's prophecy for the command of Moses, which was subsequent to the prophecy, required that the Canaanites should be exterminated, not enslaved. Was the command of Moses defeated by this act of Joshua? Certainly not; for had Joshua's act violated the command given him, it would certainly have received the divine disapprobation, which it did not receive. Joshua's act is justified by that part of the command which directed the manner in which the command was to be fulfilled; that is, the Canaanites were to be exterminated "by little and little: thou mayest not consume them at once:" therefore, the "sparing the lives" of the Gibeonites was not a violation of the command. Was the command fulfilled? It certainly was. The Gibeonites in their enslaved condition, continued subject to the burdens imposed upon them, and were "very faithful" to the Israelites until the reign of David, when they entirely ceased to exist as a distinct people; thus was the command literally fulfilled. With regard to the deferred execution of the command, we remark, that it was in perfect conformity with the divine procedure. David repented and had his punishment deferred. Hezekiah was told that he must "die and not live," but upon his "praying to the Lord," fifteen years were added to his life. So with the Gibeonites, their fidelity to the Israelites deferred their extermination, and brought it about it in a milder and more gradual form than its immediate accomplishment would have been.

Having disposed of the Gibeonites, we resume the narrative of Joshua's progress in conquering the land. After Joshua had settled the condition of the Gibeonites, Adonizedek, king of Jerusalem; Hoham, king of Hebron; Piram, king of Jarmuth; Japhia, king of Lachish, and Debir, king of Eglon, combined their forces for the purpose of fighting against the Gibeonites. Joshua marched to their assistance: "And the Lord said unto Joshua, Fear them not; for I have delivered them into thine hand: there shall not a man of them stand before thee." The battle came on, "And the Lord discomfited them before Israel, and slew them with a great slaughter at Gibeon, and chased them along the way that goeth up to Beth-horon, and smote them to Azkah, and unto Makkedah. And it came to pass as they fled from before Israel, and were in the going down to Beth-horon, that the Lord cast down great stones from heaven upon them, unto Azekah, and they died; they were more which died with hailstones than they whom the children of Israel slew with the sword."

After this Joshua took Makkedah: he destroyed the city "and all the souls that were therein; he let none remain." The same fate was realized by Libnah, and Lachish, and Eglon, and Hebron, and Debir. Joshua "destroyed all the souls that were therein: he left none remaining."

"So Joshua smote all the country of the hills, and of the south, and of the vale, and of the springs, and all their kings: he left none remaining, but utterly destroyed all that breathed, as the Lord God of Israel commanded. And Joshua smote them from Kadesh-barnea even unto Gaza, and all the country of Goshen, even unto Gibeon."

Jabin, king of Hazor, having "heard these things," sent "to Jabab, king of Madon, and to the king of Shimron, and to the king of Achshapp, and to the kings that were on the north of the mountains, and of the plains south of Chinneroth, and in the valley, and in the borders of Dor, on the west; and to the Canaanite, on the east and on the west; and to the Amorite, and to the Hittite, and the Perizzite, and the Jebusite, in the mountains; and to the Hivite, under Hermon, in the land of Mizpeh. And they went out, they and all their hosts with them, much people, even as the sand that is upon the sea-shore, in multitude." With these hosts the Israelites fought and overcame them, and "smote them until they left them none remaining." On his return from this great battle, Joshua took Hazor, and "smote all the souls that were therein, with the edge of the sword, utterly destroying them: there was not any left to breathe." All the cities of the confederated kings were taken; the Israelites "smote them with the edge of the sword, and utterly destroyed them." The spoils of these cities were preserved to the Israelites; "but every man they smote with the edge of the sword, until they had destroyed them; neither left they any to breathe,"

It is a fact, that not a city, or people, except the Gibeon-ites, sought to make terms of peace with the Israelites, all were exterminated: "For it was of the Lord to harden their hearts, that they should come against Israel in battle, that they might destroy them utterly, and that they might have no favor, but that he might destroy them, as the Lord commanded Moses."

After this Joshua proceeded against the Anakims and over-threw them: some of them escaped "in Gaza, in Gath, and in Ashdod, where they remained." These cities belonged to the Philistines (and did not fall within the limits of Joshua's con-quests); this accounts for the appearance of the Anakims after-wards among the Israelites.

It is reasonable to suppose that many of the Canaanites escaped being destroyed, by taking refuge in neighboring nations – in Africa, in Asia Minor, in Greece, and in different islands of the Ægean and Mediterranean sea; and became amalgamated with their peoples.

Section 5

Joshua commenced the conquest of the promised land A.M. 2553, and was six years engaged in its accomplishment; after which "the whole land rested from war;" that is, that portion of the land of Canaan which it was designed should be conquered by Joshua, was now in the possession of the Israelites.

Joshua having completed his conquests, was for some time engaged in dividing the conquered land among the Israelites. When that duty was performed, he said to the people, "How long are ye slack to go to possess the land, which the Lord God of your fathers hath given you?" The Israelites immediately set about the conquest of the remainder of the land; they sent out from the tribes which were to inherit it, three men each; these men were to pass through the land; "to describe it," and to report to Joshua, who was to divide it. The men sent out "described it by cities, into seven parts, in a book," and brought the book to Joshua, who divided the land. The conquest of the land being completed, after this arrangement, "the Lord gave them rest round about, according to all that he sware unto their fathers: and there stood not a man of all their enemies before them: the Lord delivered all their enemies into their hand."

There remained many of the original Canaanites scattered through the land; these were compelled to *"serve under tribute,"* and were not, like the Gibeonites, reduced to slavery. With respect to these scattered Canaanites, Joshua said to the Israelites: "Take good heed therefore, unto yourselves, that ye love the Lord your God. Else, if ye do in any wise go back, and cleave unto the remnant of these nations, even these that remain among you, and shall make marriages with them, and go in unto them, and they to you; know for a certainty that the Lord your God will no more drive out any of these nations from before you; but they shall be snares and traps unto you, and scourges in your sides, and thorns in your eyes, until ye perish from off this good land which the Lord your God hath given you." On closing this branch of the subject, it may be interesting to inquire, *Why were the Canaanites to be exterminated?* The answer to this inquiry may be read in the eighteenth and twentieth chapters of the book of Leviticus, to which we refer the reader. All the abominations contained in those chapters, and which were forbidden the Israelites, were practiced by the Canaanites. These abominations removed them beyond the range of the divine mercy! "The land itself," as if incapable of containing such sinners, "vomiteth out her inhabitants." Besides, it must be remembered that the Canaanites were to be succeeded in the promised land by a people to whom the Oracles of Salvation were being delivered, and from whom should spring the Redeemer of the world. A people thus favored should be pure and uncorrupt.

Section 6

When the Israelitish host, A. M. 2514, stood before the holy mount for the purpose of receiving the laws which were to be the rule of their conduct, as related to their worship, their civil polity, and their domestic organization, God said: "I am the Lord your God, which brought you forth out of the land of Egypt, to give you the land of Canaan, and to be your God. And if thy brother that dwelleth by thee be waxen poor, and be sold unto thee; thou shalt not compel him to serve as a bond-servant, but as a hired servant, and as a sojourner, he shall be with thee, and shall serve thee unto the year of jubilee; and then shall he depart from thee, both he and his children with him, and shall return unto his own family, and unto the possession of his fathers shall he return: for they are my servants, which I brought forth out of the land of Egypt: they shall not be sold as bondmen. Thou shalt not rule over him with rigor; but shalt fear thy God.

"Both thy bondmen and thy bondmaids, which thou shalt have, shall be of the heathen that are round about you; of them shall ye buy bondmen and bondmaids. Moreover, of the children of the strangers that do sojourn among you, of them shall ye buy, and of their families that are with you, which they begat in your land; and they shall be your possession. And ye shall take them for an inheritance for your children after you, to inherit them for a possession; they shall be your bondmen forever."

There is no possible misunderstanding the text; it contains the clearest and most explicit authority for slavery in the Church; (on which subject we shall say more in a subsequent part of this work). But slavery existed among the Israelites before this time; Josephus, in speaking of the great interest excited in the Hebrew community on the occasion of Moses giving instructions to Joshua, relative to the conquest of the promised land, says, "the very slaves were present also." These slaves the Israelites brought with them from the land of Egypt.

Had it been designed that the promised land, to which the Israelites were journeying, should, in modern language, be free soil, here is the place that we should find the command; instead of that, however, we find a command directly the reverse.

Abraham, when he was separated from his father's house, in order that he might become "the father of the faithful," that is, the father of all true believers; was authorized to purchase and possess slaves, as we shall see. And here, when his posterity had become numerous and were journeying to the promised land for the purpose of possessing it, they are informed, not only that they may possess slaves, but of whom they were to procure them, and how the slaves themselves were to be regarded; that is, as property; *"for he [the slave] is his [the master's] money."*

It will not escape the attention of the reader, that slaves were to be procured by the Israelites of the heathen. Israelitish slaves, persons reduced to poverty among them, might be purchased and possessed, but theirs was a limited servitude, which did not extend beyond the next occurring year of jubilee; and their treatment was to be that of hired-servants and not that of bond-servants: but heathen-slaves were to be a possession and an inheritance to the purchaser and his children forever.

At the first view this would appear to be an arrangement against heathen-slaves, but a little consideration will show that it was an arrangement in favor of such slaves; for these were the means by which they were to be brought to the knowledge of the true God; into his Church, and finally to salvation.

Slaves were to be procured by the Israelites, from the heathen round about them; so they have been procured by the people of the South. The slaves they possess, although natives of a distant country, were brought to their doors and sold to them, by foreigners: for the people of the South have ever had, comparatively, but a small share in their importation, as we shall see.

Let the reader turn his attention to the facts stated in the fourth and fifth chapters of this work, and he will at once see the beneficial results of slavery to the enslaved; results which shall continue to enlarge until Christianity, with all its attendant blessings, shall reach every child of Africa, whether he be found in the United States or in his native country.

We submit one other remark here – it is the design of Providence to secure the redemption of Africans by permitting them to be brought into Christian countries and Christian families. Their reclamation from heathenism has been attempted by sending white missionaries among them in their native country; but while the Church has had to deplore the loss of many valuable lives from this course, the very small amount of good accomplished shows that that arrangement was a failure. It would be gratifying to know how many missionaries have been lost by the Churches having operations in Africa. It seems to us to be but justice to the memories of these devoted men and women, that their names should be mentioned in this connection. Are there not persons sufficiently interested in this subject, who will furnish us with the facts?

Section 7

Slavery existed in Africa long before the time of Joshua, at least as early as A. M. 2083. – Terah, the father of Abraham, left Ur of the Chaldees, for the purpose of going into the land of Canaan, A. M. 2078, having Abraham in his company: he proceeded as far as Haran, where he died. A. M. 2083, the Lord said unto Abraham, who was then called Abram, "Get thee out of thy country, and from thy kindred, and from thy father's house, unto a land that I will show thee; and I will make of thee a great nation, and I will bless thee, and make thy name great; and thou shalt be a blessing: and I will bless them that bless thee, and curse him that curseth thee: and in thee shall all families of the earth be blessed."

This clear, beautiful and expressive language, arouses the attention to the fact, that some great change of affairs is now about to occur; and it keeps the attention on the alert to discover the beginnings of the anticipated event. That event was the organization of the Church. Abraham was a slave-holder at this time.

In compliance with the directions which he had received, Abraham journeyed into the land of Canaan: here the Lord appeared to him and said, "Unto thy seed will I give this land;" this promise, as we have seen, was fulfilled to the Israelites. Abraham made no permanent settlement in the land of Canaan, but continued to journey, "going on still toward the south." A famine occurring: in the land of Canaan, Abraham "went down into Egypt, to sojourn there." When he arrived near the border of Egypt, fearing the great beauty of Sarah would occasion him trouble, he directed her to pass as his sister. The matter turned out as he supposed it would, for "when Abram was come into Egypt, the Egyptians beheld the woman, that she was very fair. The princes also of Pharaoh saw her, and commended her before Pharaoh; and the woman was taken into Pharaoh's house. And he entreated Abram well for her sake; and he had sheep, and oxen, and he-asses, and men-servants, and maid-servants, and she-asses and camels." The property mentioned here, all agree, was the property of Abraham; some suppose that Abraham possessed this property previously, and carried it with him into Egypt; others think that it was given to him by Pharaoh; the latter opinion appears to us the most probable: however this may be, we learn from the statement one of two facts; namely, if Abraham carried the property with him, then he possessed slaves before he went into Egypt: if Pharaoh gave him the property, then slavery existed in Egypt before Abraham went there – let the case be the one way or the other, Abraham at this time possessed slaves. Pharaoh having returned Sarah to Abraham, he "went up out of Egypt; he, and his wife, and all that he had, and Lot with him, into the south;" that is into the southern parts of the land of Canaan. Here, we see, was slavery, long before the Gibeonites were reduced to that condition by Joshua. There is another very important fact, too, that will be noticed; namely, that slavery was introduced into the Church of God from the very beginning of its organization; for Abraham is as much to-day the "father of the faithful; the father of us all;" that is, of all faithful believers, as he was on the day when the blessings were promised to him; blessings which form the believers' inheritance to the end of the world.

Number of slaves possessed by Abraham. – A. M. 2091, certain kings confederated and made war upon the cities of Sodom and Gomorrah. Lot, "Abram's brother's son," lived in Sodom, and when the city fell into the hands of the kings, he was taken prisoner and carried away. One who had escaped from Sodom, went to Abraham and told him of the overthrow of the city and of the captivity of Lot. "And when Abraham heard that his brother was taken captive, he armed his trained servants, born in his house, three hundred and eighteen, and pursued them unto Dan;" here he joined battle with them, overcome them, and recovered all that had been lost.

A.M. 2107, after the destruction of Sodom and Gomorrah, by the angel of the Lord, Abraham, who was then in that part of the country, "journeyed from thence towards the south country, and dwelled between Kadesh and Shur, and sojourned in Gerar." Abraham being in a strange country, and fearing that he should be involved in trouble on account of Sarah, resorted to the old expedient of having her pass as his sister. "Abimelech, king of Gerar, sent and took Sarah. But God came to Abimelech, in a dream by night, and said to him. Behold, thou art but a dead man, for the woman which thou hast taken; for she is a man's wife." "And Abimelech took sheep, and oxen, and men-servants, and women-servants, and gave them unto Abraham, and restored him Sarah his wife." Here we see, that Abraham had not only the number of his slaves increased, but that slavery existed in Palestine at this time.

Isaac was a slave-holder. – "For he had possession of flocks, and possession of herds, and great store of servants. And the Philistines envied him."

Jacob was a slave-holder. – When Jacob left Mesopotamia and was returning to the promised land, expecting to meet Esau, whom he greatly feared, he sent messengers to him, "And commanded them saying, Thus shall ye speak unto my lord Esau; Thy servant Jacob saith thus: I have sojourned with Laban, and stayed there until now: and I have oxen, and asses, flocks, and men-servants, and women-servants: and I have sent to tell my lord, that I may find grace in thy sight."

Section 8

Having shown that slavery existed long before the Israelites entered the promised land, that Abraham, Isaac and Jacob were slave-holders, and having disposed of the other sons of Ham, our attention will now be directed to Cush.

CUSH; blackness, or heat. – Martindale. This definition applies as well to the people as to the country of the Cushites. Josephus asserts, "that as for the four sons of Ham, time has not at all hurt the name of Chus; for the Ethiopians, over whom he reigned, are even at this day, both by themselves and all men in Asia, called Chusites."

The term Cush, is by the Vulgate, Septuagint and other authorities, generally rendered Ethiopia; that is, *the land of Cush:* yet it must be admitted, that there are many passages which will not allow of such a rendering: notwithstanding, Ethiopia in Hebrew is frequently called Cush. That Cush and Ethiopia were terms used indifferently, to designate the same people and country, there can be no doubt.

From the fact of the Ethiopians having made settlements and removals out of Africa, much confusion has occurred among early writers. They first settled on the Persian Gulf, in Chuzestan; thence they spread over India and portions of Arabia, near the Red sea; whence the main body passed into Africa, to the south of Egypt; thence to the center of Africa; thence from increasing numbers and other causes, as is supposed, for we have no history to guide us, they continued to stretch farther south and west, until they appeared upon the coasts; where we find *"in the woolly-headed Negro the genuine Cushite."* Whenever the main body of the people emigrated, numbers remained at the place of their last settlement; it was from one of these remaining bands, doubtless, that Moses took a wife, "for he had married an Ethiopian woman."

The earliest accounts extant of the Ethiopians, show that they were gross idolaters; but it is impossible now to trace their system of idolatry, if they had a system, with any degree of certainty. From their long-continued intercourse with the Egyptians, their immediate neighborhood, and other causes, it is probable that their system received many of its features from the Egyptian, which everybody knows was of the grossest kind: however that may be, they have continued to become more and more debased, until the last trace of an idea of God has disappeared.

They have no idolatry; no legends; no sacred streams or groves; no sacrifices; no temples; no priests; no incantations; no literature; no history; no traditions; all, all, is one unbroken night of palpable darkness: no other people ever departed so far from God. In this we find the cause of the curse of Noah's prophecy.

The early discoverers of new countries have found that the aborigines have generally some well-defined idea of a Supreme Being – some tolerably correct notion of the Deity; but the Ethiopians present an exception to this rule; with them, literally and truly, "There is no God." An author says, "While Satan is obviously the author of the polytheism of other nations, he has employed his sagacity with fatal success in erasing every vestige of religious impression from their minds." The rain-maker and the gree-gree doctor, the greatest impostors among them, are the only mysterious characters with which they are acquainted.

From this point let the reader contemplate the condition of Africa, and then compare that condition with the condition of Africans in the United States, and with those sent from the United States to Liberia, and he will easily comprehend the benefits and purposes of slavery.

Section 9

Our object at present is to show, to some extent at least, the condition of the Negro in Africa, at this time. The authors we shall use for this purpose, are Denham, Clapperton, and Oudney, (officers of the army sent out by the British government, for the purpose of "solving that interesting problem [the discovery of the mouth of the Niger; afterwards accomplished by the Landers], to which the discovery of the enterprising Mungo Park gave rise." These travellers passed through Northern, starting at Tripoli, into Central Africa, as far south as Musfeia, in lat. 9° 15′ N.) and Rev. Robert Moffat, who was twenty-three years an agent of the London Missionary Society, in Southern Africa. What we take from these authors we present in the form of extracts, or quotations. We adopt this course, *first*, because they are Englishmen, not only opposed to slavery, but regarding it with feelings little short of horror; *secondly*, because their position, their writings, possess all the solemnity of official reports; not being subject to the criticisms of independent travellers. There can be entertained no possible suspicion of misstatement or exaggeration on their part; *thirdly*, because the course pursued may excite the desire for the thorough investigation of a subject too much neglected, and therefore but imperfectly understood. It will be perceived at once that from the course pursued, nothing but an imperfect sketch can be presented here; but we trust that that sketch, if well considered, will be sufficient to exhibit to the reader, facts which go to make up one of the most revolting pictures of degradation and misery that was ever presented to the mind of man.

The reader will not fail to observe that there exists a material difference in the condition of the people of Northern and Central, with those of Southern Africa, growing out of the fact, that Mahometanism with all its disgusting incidents, exists in the former, and does not exist in the latter.

Northern and Central Africa

The first thing that arrested the attention of the travellers, and continued to interest them throughout, was the operations of the institution of slavery; they say: "On the day previous to our approach to Sockna (a town about half-way between Tripoli and Mourzuk, which we reached in fourteen days), the uniformity of the journey was somewhat enlivened by meeting with a kafila of slaves from Fezzan, in which were about *seventy Negresses*, much better looking, and more healthy, than any we had seen near the sea-coast. They were marching in parties of fifteen or twenty; and on our inquiring of one of those parties from whence they came, the poor things divided themselves with the greatest simplicity, and answered, 'Souden, Begharmi, and Kanem,' pointing out the different parcels, from each country, as they spoke."

Extent of the slave market of Mourzuk. "You pass through the *fsug* (slave market) a wide street, with houses on each side, *three hundred yards in length.*"

"We had a fsug, or market, in front of one of the principal gates of the town (Kouka); *slaves*, sheep and bullocks, the latter in great numbers, were the principal live stock for sale."

Boo-Khaloom, (a slave merchant). – "He was represented to us, and truly, as a merchant of very considerable riches and influence in the interior. He was on the eve of starting for Tripoli, from Mourzuk, with really superb presents for the bashaw. He had *five hundred slaves*, the handsomest that could be procured, besides other things."

The Sultan of Mourzuk. – "It was not till the 18th that the sultan, after attending the Mosque, started for Tripoli; all his camels and suite had marched in divisions, for three days previous – *in slaves he had alone, more than one thousand five hundred.*"

Capturing slaves. – "The sultan of Mandara had given no intimation whatever of his intentions with regard to Boo-Khaloom's destination, and in consequence, the impatience and discontent of the latter were extreme. Offerings poured in from all the Kerdy nations (Negroes who have not embraced the Mahometan faith); and the sultan excused himself to Boo-Khaloom for the delay, on account of the extreme tractability of the people around him, who he said were becoming Musselmans without force. Again Musgow was mentioned; adding, that the warlike arm of the Arabs, bearing the sword of the prophet, might turn their hearts. This hypocrisy, however, Boo-Khaloom inveighed against most loudly to me, declaring that the conversion of the Kerdy people would lose him (the sultan) thousands of slaves, as their constant wars with each other afforded them the means of supplying him abundantly."

One of the travellers speaking of his arrival at the palace of the sultan of Mandara, and of his desire to visit the neighboring mountains, says: "I was conducted into the presence of the chief eunuch; he desired me to stop within about twelve yards of him, and then said, 'The sultan could not imagine what I wanted at the hills. Did I wish to catch the Kerdies alone? – that I had better buy them, – he would sell me *as many as I pleased.*' I assured him that I did not wish to go at all to the hills if the sultan had the slightest objection, that it was purely curiosity; and that as to catching Kerdies, I would not take them if given to me."

The taking of the Kerdy town of Dirkulla, is thus related: "On emerging from the wood, the large Felatah of Dirkulla was perceivable, and the Arabs were formed in front, headed by Boo-Khaloom: they were flanked on each side by a large body of cavalry; and as they moved on, shouting the Arab war-cry, which is very inspiring, I thought I could perceive a smile between Barca Gana and the chiefs, at Boo-Khaloom's expense. Dirkulla was quickly burnt, and another small town near it; and the few inhabitants that were found in them, who were chiefly infants and aged persons, unable to escape, *were put to death without mercy, or thrown into the flames.*"

A lengthy account, of which the preceding paragraph is the commencement, is closed thus: "Boo-Khaloom's imprudence in having suffered himself to be persuaded to attack the Felatahs became now apparent, as although in case of his overcoming them, he might have appropriated to himself all the slaves, both male and female, that he found amongst them; yet the Felatahs themselves were Moslem, and he could not have made them slaves."

Alluding to a people called Munga, who were difficult to be controlled by the shieks, although Musselmen, it is said: "Another complaint against the Mongowy was, that they were kaffering and not saying their prayers! the dogs. This is, however, a fault which is generally laid to the charge of any nation against whom a true Musselman wages war, as it gives him the power of making them slaves. By the laws of Mahomet, one believer must not bind another."

"The town of Kabshary, where we halted, had been nearly destroyed by the Mongowy. On attacking a place, it is the custom of the country instantly to fire it; and as they are all composed of straw huts only, the whole is shortly devoured by the flames. The unfortunate inhabitants fly quickly from the destructive element, and fall immediately into the hands of their no less merciless enemies, who surround the place. The men are quickly massacred, and the women and children lashed together and made slaves."

A reconnoitering party had gone out, and "about three in the afternoon they began to return, bringing with them women and children of both sexes, to the amount of eight hundred. One Shouaa, a friend of mine, brought a poor woman with four children, two in her arms, and two on the father's horse, who had been stabbed for defending those he held most dear upon earth."

Gangs of slaves. – "No kafila is permitted to enter Kouka during the sheikah's absence, nor dare the merchants offer any goods for sale till they have his permission. On this account, one consisting of ten merchants from Soudan, was ordered to encamp at a short distance from us, and await the movements of the army. They had nearly a hundred slaves, the greater part female, girls of from twelve to eighteen years of age, some of them from Nyffee, and still farther to the west, of a deep copper color, and beautifully formed; but few of these were ironed. The males, who were mostly young, were linked together in couples by iron rings round their legs; yet they laughed, and seemed in good condition."

"It is a common practice with the merchants to induce one slave to persuade his companions, that on arriving at Tripoli, they will be free, and clothed in red, a color all Negroes are passionately fond of; by which promises they are induced to submit quietly, until they are too far from their homes to render escape possible but at the risk of starvation. If the hundreds, nay thousands of skeletons that whiten in the blast between this place [Kouka] and Mourzuk did not, of themselves, tell a tale replete with woe, the difference of appearance in all slaves here (where they are fed tolerably), and the state in which they usually arrive in Fezzan, would but too clearly prove the acuteness of the sufferings which commence on their leaving the negro country."

"Two kafilas passed us to-day, on their way to Kouka. They consisted of one hundred and fifty slaves, with about twenty merchants and their servants, and thirty camels. Most of the people ran to the outskirts of the camp to see them pass, it being the custom on these occasions, to dress out these poor victims of the most cruel avarice that certainly ever entered into the breast of man, in rags of different colors, only to be taken from them again on the procession being over. The merchants, who gratify their vanity the most in this way, lose, it is said, fewer slaves; but I observed several of these before me, whose unbidden tears flowed down their cheeks as they drew their mantles close round them, seeming to wish by that means to stifle their misery with the appearance of it."

A plundering party. – A plundering excursion among the Begharmi by the sheikh of Kouka, is thus related: "The plunder was said to have amounted to four hundred and eighty horses, and nearly two hundred women, with two eunuchs, and the baggage of the princes, which was carried on bullocks and asses. Fifty of their women were *sirias* [slaves worthy of being admitted into the seraglio], of great beauty, belonging to the sultan's sons, and these were all given up to the sheikh. When the rejoicing for the victory began to abate a little, the fsug was crowded with slaves taken from the Begharmi, and they were cheap in proportion to their numbers. I saw several fine boys and girls sold for two or three bullocks – ten dollars. And a shouaa was extremely anxious for the red cap on my head, for which, with an old muslin turban, he offered me a very pretty girl, about fourteen years old."

"When I appeared before the sultan" [of Angala], says one of the travellers, "he examined me very minutely, when the shade was again drawn. I begged for permission to embark on the Shary, and was told he would consider of it. He particularly inquired if I wished to purchase *b'lowy*, or handsome female slaves, which I assured him I did not; 'because,' said he, 'if you do, go no further: I have some hundreds, and will sell them to you as cheap as any one.'"

Employments of female slaves. – "There are a particular class of female slaves here [Kouka] to whom the duty of watching and laboring in the fields of grain is always allotted. I have before said, that all laborious work is performed by that sex we consider as the weakest, and whom we employ in the more domestic duties only – and it is to them this perilous work is assigned. The female slaves from Musgow are never bought by the Tripoli or Fezzan traders: their features, naturally large and ugly, are so much disfigured by the silver stud which they wear in the under lip, that no purchaser would be found for them; besides the loss of the two front teeth, which are punched out to make way for the silver, which goes quite through into their mouths, the weight of the metal, after a year or two, drags the lip down, so as to make it quite lie on the chin, and gives a really frightful appearance to the face. These poor creatures, therefore, who are generally of a strong make, and patient under their sufferings, guard the crops and collect the harvest, and a year seldom passes without several of them being snatched away by lions, who, crouching under cover of the ripening corn, spring on their prey and bear it off."

Sports. – "Since the feast day of the Aid Kebir, there had been, on an evening, an assembly of persons before the shiekh's gate [at Kouka], when the most athletic and active of the slaves came out and wrestled in the presence of their masters and the shiekh himself, who usually took his post at a little window over the principal gate of the palace. Barca Gana, Ali Gana, Wormah, Tirab, and all the chiefs, were usually seated on mats in the inner ring, and I generally took my place beside them. Quickness and main strength were the qualifications which insured victory; they struggled with a bitterness which could scarcely have been exceeded in the armed contests of the Roman gladiators, and which was greatly augmented by the voices of their masters urging them to the most strenuous exertion of their powers. A rude trumpet of the buffalo's horn sounded to the attack, and the combatants entered the arena naked, with the exception of a leathern girdle about the loins; and those who had been victorious on former occasions were received with loud acclamations by the spectators. Slaves of all nations were first matched against each other; of these, the natives of Soudan were the least powerful, and seldom victors. The most arduous struggles were between the Musgowy and the Begharmi negroes. Some of these slaves, and particularly the latter, were beautifully formed, and of gigantic stature; but the feats of the day always closed by the matching of two Begharmis against each other, and dislocated limbs or death were often the consequence of these kindred encounters. They commence by placing their hands on each other's shoulders; of their feet they make no use, but frequently stoop down, and practice a hundred deceptions, to throw the adversary off his guard; when the other will seize his antagonist by the hips, and, after holding him in the air, dash him against the ground with stunning violence, where he lies covered with blood, and unable to pursue the contest. I have seen them foam and bleed at the mouth and nose from pure rage and exertion, their owners all the time vying with each other in using expressions most likely to excite their fury: one chief will draw a pistol, and swear by the Koran that his slave shall not survive an instant his defeat, and with the same breath offer him great rewards if he conquers. Both of these promises are sometimes too faithfully kept; and one poor wretch, who had withstood the attacks of a ponderous Negro, much more than his match, from some country to the south of Mandara, for more than fifty minutes, turned his eye reproachfully on his threatening master only for an instant, when his antagonist slipped his hands down from the shoulders to the loins, and, by a sudden twist, raised his knee to his chest, and fell with his whole weight on the poor slave (who was from Soudan), snapping his spine in the fall."

Hardships of Slaves. – "The depth of the well at Meshroo is from sixteen to twenty feet; the water good, and free from saline impregnations. The ground around is strewed with human skeletons, the slaves who have arrived, exhausted with thirst and fatigue. The horrid consequences of the slave trade were strongly brought to our mind; and although its horrors are not equal to those of the European trade, still they are sufficient to call up every sympathy, and rouse up every spark of humanity. They are dragged over deserts, water often fails, and provisions scarcely provided for the long and dreary journey. The Moors ascribe the numbers to the cruelty of the Tibboo traders: there is perhaps too much truth in the accusation. Every few miles a skeleton was seen, through the whole day; some were partially covered with sand, others with only a small mound, formed by the wind; one hand often lay under the head, and frequently both, as if in the act of compressing the head. The skin and membranous substance all shrivelled up and dry from the state of the air: the thick muscular and internal parts only decay."

"About sunset we baited near a well, within half a mile of Meshroo. Round this spot were lying more than one hundred skeletons, some of them with the skin still remaining attached to the bones – not even a little sand thrown over them. The Arabs laughed heartily at my expression of horror, and said, 'they were only blacks, *nam hoo!'* [damn their fathers!] and began knocking about the limbs with the butt-end of their firelocks, saying, 'This was a woman! this was a youngster!' and such like unfeeling expressions. I was assured that they had left Bornou with not above a quarter's allowance for each; and that more died from want than fatigue. They were marched off with chains round their necks and legs. The most robust only arrived in Fezzan in a very debilitated state, and were there fattened for the Tripoli slave market. Our camels did not come up until it was quite dark, and we bivouacked in the midst of these unearthed remains of the victims of persecution and avarice, after a long day's journey of twenty-six miles, in the course of which one of our party counted one hundred and seven of these skeletons."

"One of the skeletons we passed to-day had a very fresh appearance; the beard was still hanging to the skin of the face, and the features were still discernible. A merchant travelling with the kafila suddenly exclaimed, 'That was my slave! I left him behind four months ago, near this spot.' 'Make haste, take him to the *fsug'* [market], said an Arab wag, 'for fear anybody else should claim him.'"

"Skeletons lay about, mangled in a shocking manner; here a leg, there an arm, fixed with their ligaments, at considerable distances from the trunk."

"During the last two days we had passed, on an average, from sixty to eighty or ninety skeletons each day; but the numbers that lay about the wells at El-Hammar were countless. Those of two women, whose perfect and regular teeth bespoke them young, were particularly shocking; their arms still remained clasped round each other as they had expired, although the flesh had long since perished, by being exposed to the burning rays of the sun, and the blackened bones only left. The nails of the fingers, and some of the sinews of the hand, also remained, and part of the tongue of one of them still appeared through the teeth."

Southern Africa

Ignorance, subjection, filthiness, &c. – Speaking of the Balalas (poor ones among the Bechuana tribes), Moffat says: "Though in general, they are able to state to what chief or tribe they belong, yet from want of intercourse, and from desolating wars, which are only waged where there is prospect of plunder, great numbers of them become, in their isolated position, independent. They are never permitted to keep cattle, and are exposed to the caprice, cupidity and tyranny of the town-lords, whenever they happen to come in their way. They live a hungry life, being dependent on the chase, wild roots, berries, locusts, and, indeed, anything eatable that comes within their reach; and when they have a more than usual supply, they will bury it in the earth, from their superiors, who are in the habit of taking [from them] what they please. Resistance on their part would be instantly avenged with the deadly javelin. When hunting parties go out to kill game, the Belala, men and women, are employed to carry grievous burdens of flesh to the rendezvous of the hunters; in return for which, they receive the offals of the meat, and are made drudges, so long as the party remains. They are never permitted to wear the furs of foxes and other animals they obtain. The flesh they may eat; but the skins are conveyed to the towns, for which they obtain a small piece of tobacco, or an old spear or knife. Indeed, all the valuable skins of the larger animals, which they sometimes procure by hunting and pitfalls, as well as the better portions of the meat, they have to yield to their nominal masters, except when they succeed in secreting the whole, for their own use. Their servile state, their scanty clothing, their exposure to the inclemency of the weather, and their extreme poverty, have, as may be easily conceived, a deteriorating influence on their character and condition. They are generally less in stature, and though not deficient in intellect, the life they lead gives a melancholy cast to their features, and from constant intercourse with beasts of prey and serpents in their path, as well as exposure to harsh treatment, they appear shy, and have a wild, and frequently suspicious look. Nor can this be wondered at, when it is remembered that they associate with savage beasts, from the lion that roams abroad by night and day, to the deadly serpent which infests their path, keeping them always on the alert, during their perambulations. All this, and much more, which might be said of the Balala, may also, with the strictest propriety, be affirmed of the Bushmen."

The following extract is by no means to be confined to any particular class, but will apply to all: "When Mr. Hamilton arrived at Flose Fountain, two days' journey south of our station on the Kuruman, a circumstance occurred which may be noticed, were it only to show what human beings are in certain situations. Halting at the above place in the evening, a dead horse was found that had belonged to one of the Griquas, and which had been killed by the bite of a serpent. Next morning the women fell on the swollen and half putrid carcase, and began, like so many wolves, to tear it limb from limb; every one securing as much as she could for herself. Mr. H., who looked on with utter amazement, advised them to avoid the part where the animal was bitten. To his friendly warning they paid no attention whatever; in the space of about an hour a total dissection was effected, and every particle of skin, meat, bone, the entrails and their contents, were carried off. Mr. H. was obliged to remain the whole day, finding it absolutely impossible to induce them to leave the spot till every particle was devoured, and in the evening they actually danced and sang with joy." There was no necessity for this, for the people were allowed a regular supply of rations by the missionary.

Inhumanity to Children. – Kicherer says: "Their manner of life is extremely wretched and disgusting. They delight to be-smear their bodies with the fat of animals, mingled with ochre, and sometimes with grime. They are utter strangers to cleanliness, as they never wash their bodies, but suffer the dirt to accumulate, so that it will hang a considerable length from their elbows. They are total strangers to domestic happiness. The men have several wives [slaves], but conjugal affection is little known. They take no great care of their children, and never correct them except in a fit of rage, when they almost kill them by severe usage."

"Tame Hottentots seldom destroy their children, except in a fit of passion; but the Bushmen will kill their children without remorse, on various occasions – as when they are ill-shaped; when they are in want of food; when the father of a child has forsaken its mother, &c., in which case they will strangle them, smother them, cast them away in the desert, or bury them alive."

Inhumanity to Parents. – "Among the poorer classes, it is indeed struggling for existence; and when the aged become too weak to provide for themselves, and are a burden to those whom they brought forth and reared to manhood, they are not unfrequently abandoned by their own children, with a meal of victuals and a cruse of water, to perish in the desert. I have seen a small circle of stakes fastened in the ground, within which were still lying the bones of a parent, bleaching in the sun, who had been thus abandoned. In one instance, I observed a small broken earthenware vessel, in which the last draught of water had been left. 'What is this,' I said, pointing to the stakes, addressing Africaner. His reply was, 'This is heathenism;' and then described this parricidal custom." Mr. Moffat thus describes another in-stance of this kind, in a different stage of progress: 'On reaching the spot, we beheld an object of heart-rending distress. It was a venerable-looking old woman, a living skeleton, sitting, with her head leaning on her knees. She appeared terrified at our presence, and especially at me. She tried to rise, but trembling with weakness, sunk again to the earth. I addressed her by the name which sounds sweet in every clime, and charms even the savage ear: 'My mother, fear not, we are friends, and will do you no harm.' I put several questions to her, but she appeared either speechless, or afraid to open her lips. I again repeated, 'Pray, mother, who are you, and how do you come to be in this situation?' To which she replied, 'I am a woman. I have been here four days; my children have left me here to die!' 'Your children!' I interrupted. 'Yes,' raising her hand to her shrivelled bosom, 'my own children, three sons and two daughters. They are gone,' pointing with her finger, 'to yonder blue mountain, and have left me to die.' 'And pray, why did they leave you?' I inquired. Spreading out her hands, 'I am old, you see, and am no longer able to serve them; when they kill game, I am too feeble to help in carrying home the flesh; I am not able to gather wood to make fire; and I cannot carry their children on my back, as I used to do.' I remarked that I was surprised that she had escaped the lions, which seemed to abound, and to have approached very near the spot where she was. She took hold of the skin of her left arm with her fingers, and raising it up, as one would do a loose linen, she added, 'I hear the lions, but there is nothing on me that they would eat; I have no flesh on me for them to scent.' I have often reasoned with the natives on this cruel practice, in reply to which they would only laugh!"

Propensity to steal, &c. – "As many men and women as pleased, might come into our hut, leaving us not room even to turn ourselves, and making everything they touched the color of their own greasy, red attire; while some were talking, others would be sleeping, and some pilfering whatever they could lay their hands upon. This would keep a housewife a perfect prisoner, in a suffocating atmosphere, almost intolerable; and when they departed they left ten times more than their number behind – company still more offensive. As it was not pleasant to take our meals amongst such filth, our dinner was often deferred for hours, hoping for their departure; but, after all, it had to be eaten when the natives were despatching their game at our feet. Our attendance at public worship would vary from one to forty; and these very often manifested the greatest indecorum. Some would be snoring; others laughing; some working; and others, who might even be styled the noblesse, would be employed in removing from their ornaments certain nameless insects, letting them run about the forms, while sitting by the missionary's wife. Never having been accustomed to chairs or stools, some, by way of imitation, would sit with their feet on the benches, having their knees, according to their usual mode of sitting, drawn up to their chins. In this position, one would fall asleep and tumble over, to the great merriment of his fellows. On some occasions an opportunity would be watched to rob, when the missionary was engaged in public service. The thief would just put his head within the door, discover who was in the pulpit, and knowing he could not leave his rostrum before a certain time had elapsed, would go to his house and take what he could lay his hands upon. Some nights, or rather mornings, we had to record thefts committed in the course of twenty-four hours, in our houses, our smith-shop, our garden, and among our cattle in the field."

War. – There are incessant wars waged between the different tribes. These wars are engaged in, without provocation in general, and for the simple reason that one party desires to possess the property and persons (whom they enslave) of another – the spoils furnish the inducement. On these occasions, the utmost cruelty is observed by the conquering party. Alluding to one of these plundering excursions, which, however, was unfortunate, Moffat says: "It was afterwards discovered that the enemy had resolutely determined to kill, as well as to steal, and set the place on fire, which they used their utmost exertions to accomplish. Having heard that this party had, in their course, deliberately murdered all the unoffending natives who had fallen into their hands, I inquired of the prisoners after they had been some time with us, if their minds never revolted at such crimes, as deliberately killing innocent females and children, who possessed nothing to tempt their cupidity, but who had cheerfully served them with wood and water. I shall never forget the reply of one, who, after sitting some minutes motionless in deep reflection, said, 'Mynheer, the heart of man is a wonderful thing; there is nothing; which it cannot do. Custom makes even murder a plaything.'"

We present the following as a common instance of their barbarity after a battle: "The wounded enemy they baited with stones, clubs, and spears, accompanied with yellings and countenances indicative of fiendish joy. The helpless women found no quarter, especially if they possessed anything like ornaments to tempt the cupidity of their plunderers. A few copper rings round the neck, from which it was difficult to take them, was the signal for the already uplifted battle-axe to sever the head from the trunk, or the arm from the body, when the plunderer would grasp, with a smile, his bloody trophies. Others, in order to be able to return home with the triumph of victory, would pursue the screaming boy or girl, and not satisfied with severing a limb from the human frame, would exhibit their contempt for the victims of their cruel revenge, by seizing the head and hurling it from them, or kicking it to a distance."

Murder. – "I was in the habit of concluding, from facts about which I have not deemed it necessary to be very minute, that the Batlapis were, as a people, not only very ignorant and depraved, but exceedingly brutal: however, a short stay among the Barolongs convinced me that the latter far exceeded the former. An intelligent traveller (Dr. Burchell), was not mistaken, when he was obliged, most reluctantly, to come to the conclusion, that 'the foulest blot on their character, is the indifference with which murder is viewed among them. It excites little sensation, except in the family of the person who has been murdered; and brings, it is said, no disgrace upon him who has committed it; nor uneasiness, excepting the fear of their revenge.' During my stay at Kongke, an instance occurred confirming the view of Dr. Burchell. A man was quarrelling with his wife about a very trifling affair, when in a fit of rage he grasped his spear, and laid her at his feet a bleeding corpse! Here there were no coroners, nor jury, to take cognizance of the fact, and he walked about without a blush, while the lifeless body was dragged out to be devoured by the hyenas. When I endeavored to represent to the chiefs, with whom I was familiar, as old acquaintances, the magnitude of such crimes, they laughed, I might say inordinately, at the horror I felt for the murder of a woman by her own husband!"

Speaking of Moselekatse, a king, a very cruel man, Moffat says: "When I recommended a system which would secure not only safety, but plenty to his people, without the unnatural one of keeping up a force of many thousands of unmarried warriors, he tried to convince me that his people were happy, and to a stranger they might appear so, for alas, they dared not let any murmur reach his ear; but I knew more than he was aware of. I knew many a couch was steeped with silent tears, and many an acre stained with human blood. About ten minutes after the conversation, a lovely boy, a son of one of his many wives, sat smiling on my knee, caressing me as if I were his father. As some of the king's harem was seated near, I asked the boy which was his mother. He shook his little head and sighed. I asked no more, but learned soon after that the mother, who was the daughter of a captive chief, was a superior woman, and took the liberty of remonstrating with her lord on the multitude of his concubines. In the morning she was dragged out of her house, and her head severed from her body."

Polygamy. – This disgusting and abominable vice, than which none is better calculated to debauch the heart, prevails all over Africa, among all ranks, from the highest to the lowest. Alluding to the difficulties with which the missionary is embarrassed, this is reckoned as one of the most formidable. Moffat says: "Polygamy was another obstacle, and the Bechuanas, jealous of any diminution in their self-indulgence, by being deprived of the services of their wives [who are the slaves of their husbands], looked with an extremely suspicious eye on any innovation on this ancient custom. The men, for obvious reasons, found it convenient to have a number of such vassals, rather than only one, while the woman would be perfectly amazed at one's ignorance, were she to be told that she would be much happier in a single state, or widowhood, than being the mere concubine and drudge of a haughty husband, who spent the greater part of his life in lounging in the shade, while she was compelled, for his comfort, as well as her own, to discharge the heavier task of agriculture, building the houses, fencing, bringing fire-wood; and heavier than all, nature's charge, the rearing of a family." Lynch says: "Polygamy is universal, the number of wives being the measure of a man's wealth." It is easy to perceive that this custom is supported by the women, from the consideration that the larger the number of wives a husband may have, the greater division there must be of the burdens imposed upon them. This not only reconciles them to the custom, but prompts them to urge it upon their husbands.

No Religion. – Dr. Vanderkemp says: "If by religion we mean reverence for God, or the external action by which that reverence is expressed, I never could perceive that they had any religion, nor any idea of the existence of a God. I am speaking nationally, for there are many individuals who have some notion of His existence, which they have received from adjacent nations." This idea of God, possessed by adjacent nations, and communicated to the Kafirs, about whom Dr. V. is writing, is distinctly traceable to the teachings of missionaries. What is related here of the Kafirs, "will equally apply to the Hottentots and Namaques, who are one people:" indeed, it will apply to all the people of Southern Africa.

The native mind does not seem, in its uncultivated condition, to possess the ability of entertaining an idea of the Divine Being: for sometimes after hours of patient exertion on the part of the missionary to convey this idea, he would be perplexed with the question, asked with a most vacant stare, "What is it you wish to tell me?" "Inquiring one day of a group of natives whom I had been addressing, if any of them had previously known that Great Being which had been described to them, among the whole party I found only one old woman, who said that she remembered hearing the name Morimo (Molimo, according to native pronunciation, the terra adopted by the missionaries for God), when she was a child, but was not told what the thing was."

A chief one day, attending the instructions of a missionary,

after listening attentively for some time, exclaimed with amazement, "that a man whom he accounted wise, should vend such
fables for truths. Calling about thirty of his men who stood near
him, to approach, he addressed them, pointing to me, 'There is
Ra-Mary (father of Mary), who tells me that the heavens were
made, the earth also, by a beginner, whom he calls Morimo. Have
you ever heard anything to be compared with this? He says that
the sun rises and sets by the power of Morimo; as also, that
Morimo causes winter to follow summer; the winds to blow; the
rain to fall; the grass to grow, and the trees to bud; and casting his
arm above and around him, added, God works in everything you
see or hear! Did you ever hear such words?' Seeing them ready to
burst with laughter, he said, 'Wait, I shall tell you more; Ra-Mary
tells me that we have spirits in us, which will never die; and that
our bodies, though dead and buried, will rise and live again. Open
your eyes to-day; did you ever hear *litlamane* (fables) like these?'
This was followed by a burst of deafening laughter, and on its
partially subsiding, the chief man begged me to say no more on
such trifles, lest the people should think me mad."

Mr. Schmelin, a missionary among the Namaquas, says:
"After service, I spent some time conversing with the aged, but
found them extremely ignorant; some of them could not conceive
of a being higher than man, and had not the least idea of the immortality of the soul."

Africaner being asked by Mr. Campbell, "what his views
of God were before he enjoyed the benefit of Christian instruction? replied, that he never thought anything at all on these subjects; that he thought about nothing but his cattle. He admitted
that he had heard of a God (well might he, being brought up in the
colony), but at the same time stated that his views of God were so
erroneous, that the name suggested no more to his mind than
something that might be found in the form of an insect, or in the
lid of a snuff-box."

Mr. Anderson says: "When I went among the Griquas, and
for some time after, they were without the smallest marks of civilization. If I except one woman (who had by some means got a tri-

fling article of colonial raiment), they had not one thread of European clothing among them; and their wretched appearance and habits were such as might have excited in our minds an aversion to them, had we not been actuated by principles which led us to pity them, and served to strengthen us in pursuing the object of our missionary work; they were, in many instances, little above the brutes."

Relative to the Bechuanas, Moffat says: "When we attempted to convince them of their state as sinners, they would boldly affirm, with full belief in their innate rectitude, that there was not a sinner in the tribe; referring us to other nations whom they dreaded, or with whom they were at war; and especially the poor despised Bushmen." Our author continues: "I often feel at a loss what to say relative to the kingdom of Christ, at this station. A sameness marks the events of each returning day. No conversions; no inquiry after God; no objections raised to exercise our powers in defence. Indifference and stupidity, form the wreath on every brow – ignorance, the grossest ignorance of divine things, forms the basis of every action; it is only things earthly, sensual and devilish, which stimulate to activity and mirth, while the great subject of the soul's redemption appears to them like an old and ragged garment, possessing neither loveliness nor worth. We preach, we converse, we catechise, we pray, but without the least apparent success. Only satiate their mendicant spirits by perpetually giving, and we are all that is good, but refuse to meet their demands, their praises are turned to ridicule and abuse."

Alluding to Makaba, king of the Bauangketsi, he says: "Sitting down beside this great man, illustrious for war and conquest, I stated to him that my object was to tell him my news. His countenance lighted up, hoping to hear of feats of war, destruction of tribes, and such like subjects, so congenial to his savage disposition. When he found that my topics had solely a reference to the Great Being of whom, the day before, he had told me he knew nothing; and of the Saviour's mission to this world, whose name he said he had never heard, he resumed his knife and jackall's skin, and hummed a native air. One of his men, sitting near me, appeared struck with the character of the Redeemer, which I was endeavoring to describe, and particularly with His miracles. On hearing that He raised the dead, he very naturally exclaimed, What an excellent doctor he must have been, to make dead men live!"

On visiting a village of the Barolongs, Moffat "talked to them to convince them that there was something else beyond eating and drinking, which ought to command their attention. This was to them inexplicable, while the description I gave of the character of God, and our sinful and helpless condition, amused them only, and extorted some expressions of sympathy, that a *khosi* (king), as they called me, should talk such foolishness. My preaching and speaking did, indeed, appear to be casting seed by the way side, or on the flinty rock, while they would gravely ask if I were in earnest, and believed that there was such a Being as I described? It was indeed painful to hear them turning the theme of man's redemption and the Cross into ridicule, and making sport of immortality." So gross was the ignorance of the people of Southern Africa that Mr. Moffat seems strongly inclined to doubt the great truth of the innate and intuitive ideas of natural light; or, more properly, natural religion. He says: "I had with me one of the best interpreters, himself a child of God, and tried one native after another, to make my own point good [that is, to establish the fact that the human mind has in it, under all circumstances, some idea of the supreme Being]: sometimes I would even put words into the mouth of Africaner, and ask, 'Does he not mean so and so?' In some there was a glimmering of light; but again, I found to my mortification, that this had been received from the 'hat-wearers,' as they called the people from the south, or from Mr. Schmelin's station at Bethany, whom they denominated, 'the people that talked about God.'" We do not see in this, or in anything else connected with the Negroes of Africa, any reason to doubt the great truth alluded to, and which is asserted by all theologians. The case of the Negroes of Africa, in this regard, is only an exception to the general rule. "We see, in these people, not only mental, but physical peculiarities, which distinguish them from all other peoples, which peculiarities suffice to show, both the extent of their wickedness and the extent of the curse of Noah's prophecy. This explanation appears to us to be perfectly satisfactory; it maintains the generally entertained idea of natural religion, and exhibits the reason for the ignorance of the African Negroes on divine subjects.

Here we close our extracts, directing the reader to the perusal of the authors from whom they were taken, if he desires to have a perfect knowledge of African slavery and African ignorance, as they exist at this day.

In this chapter we have traced the Ham family, showing the fate of its respective branches. We have shown the establishment of slavery and its cause. We have shown that slavery existed before the organization of the Church, with Abraham and his posterity. Our duty, in the next chapter, will be to show the regulation of slavery.

CHAPTER TWO
Regulation of Slavery

Section 1

Slavery in the Church, contemporaneous with its organization. – The Bible teaches that Abraham and his household were the first members of the Church of God, under its present organization. There can be nothing, therefore, more interesting than to inquire who composed that household. The Bible says, "And Abraham took Sarai his wife, and Lot his brother's son, and all their substance that they had gathered, and the souls they had gotten in Haran: and they went forth to go into the land of Canaan, and into the land of Canaan they came."

That the words, "and the souls they had gotten in Haran," mean slaves, no one can for a moment doubt. Both Jewish and Christian commentators agree in this explanation. Jenks, in the *Comprehensive Commentary*, says, "They took with them the souls they had gotten; that is, the servants they had bought; part of their substance, but called souls to remind masters that their servants have souls, precious souls, which they ought to take care of and provide for." This must be regarded as the natural and correct import of the words under consideration; they are incapable of sustaining any other interpretation. That this view is correct, will be seen by its conformity to other instructions given to Abraham.

Circumcision. – Circumcision was an ordinance which God established in the Church at the time of its organization: "And God said unto Abraham, Thou shalt keep my covenant therefore; thou, and thy seed after thee, in their generations. This is my covenant which ye shall keep between me and you, and thy seed after thee; Every man-child among you shall be circumcised. And ye shall circumcise the flesh of your foreskin; and it shall be a token of the covenant betwixt me and you."

Subjects of Circumcision. – "And he that is eight days old, shall be circumcised among you; every man-child in your genera-tions; *he that is born in thy house, or bought with money of any stranger, which is not of thy seed.* He that is born in thy house, and he that is bought with thy money, must needs be circumcised: and my covenant shall be in your flesh, for an everlasting cove-nant."

Commands so explicit could not be misunderstood; they were faithfully obeyed. Abraham is to be regarded as standing in the midst of a sinful world, "The friend of God." There is much in this divine arrangement to call forth our gratitude and thankfulness – more particularly that provision which is made for slaves becom-ing partakers of the faith of Abraham, or in the covenant made with him. The duty is here imposed upon the parent of consecrat-ing his infant child to God, and upon the master of, in like manner, consecrating his infant slave. The duty imposed allows of no dif-ference between the parent and the master; both are under the same obligation.

This arrangement has no respect to condition, and contem-plates the dedication of all children to God; for all children should be reared in the Church.

In obedience to the command, "Abraham took Ishmael his son, *and all that were born in his house, and that were bought with his money;* every male among the men of Abraham's house, and circumcised the flesh of their foreskin, in the self-same day, as God had said unto him.

"And Abraham was ninety years old and nine, when he was

circumcised in the flesh of his foreskin. And Ishmael his son, was thirteen years old, when he was circumcised in the flesh of his foreskin.

"And all the men of his house, *born in the house, and bought with money of the stranger,* were circumcised with him."

The rite of circumcision as here established, completed the organization of the Church. The rite included, as we have seen, parent and child, master and slave. This ordinance was, by our Lord and Saviour Jesus Christ, after His resurrection, changed to that of baptism; the subjects of the ordinance, however, remained as at first. Hence, theologians deduce and teach infant baptism.

These points being ascertained, they distinctly display the obligations masters are under of consecrating their infant slaves to God; that is, of bringing them into the Church that they may be placed directly under the influence of religious training. We know of no master in or out of the Church who would forbid his adult slave becoming a member of the Church; but do masters have their infant slaves baptized into the church? Many do; but truth requires us to say that this very plain duty is too much neglected, though but few comparatively oppose it. It is no uncommon occurrence for masters out of the Church to provide the means necessary for their slaves' moral and religious instruction. Masters everywhere understand the benefit to themselves, at least of their slaves becoming religious. In this is plainly seen the workings of Providence in the direction of the great purpose, now being accomplished through the agency of slavery.

The Passover. – After the Israelites had left the land of Egypt, God established in the Church another ordinance, called the Passover. Particular directions were given to Moses, the leader of the Israelites, how this feast, often called the feast of unleavened bread, should be prepared and eaten.

Who were allowed to partake of the Passover. – "And the Lord said unto Moses and Aaron, This is the ordinance of the passover: There shall no stranger eat thereof: *but every man's servant that is bought for money, when thou hast circumcised him, then shall he eat thereof.* A foreigner and an hired servant shall not eat thereof. In one house shall it be eaten: thou shalt not carry forth aught of the flesh abroad out of the house; neither shall ye break a bone thereof. All the congregation of Israel shall keep it. And when a stranger shall sojourn with thee, and will keep the passover to the Lord, let all his males be circumcised, and then let him come near and keep it; and he shall be as one that is born in the land: for no uncircumcised person shall eat thereof. One law shall be to him that is home-born, and unto the stranger that sojourneth among you."

This ordinance (like that of circumcision) was changed by our Saviour on the night of His betrayal, into the ordinance now observed in the Church, known as the sacrament of the Lord's Supper. Here, too, it will be observed, that the change of the ordinance did not affect those who were previously qualified to partake of it. Masters and slaves had the same right in each instance.

Why was there a distinction made between a *hired* servant and a *bond* servant, with regard to the Passover? For the most obvious reasons. The arrangement of the Israelitish families, was eminently patriarchal: now a hired servant, whose presence was but occasional, was not so identified with the particular family, as to be under the government and control of its head, in the observance of the Mosaic law. It is just so now; the rule is not altered in the least: the head of the family, the master, is the patriarch of the family – the hired servants that he may occasionally employ, are not regarded as of his family, therefore he cannot require of them religious observances. But with a slave, the whole case is changed – that kind of servant is permanently in the family, and his religious training may be required; hence, the master's responsibility.

The Moral Law. – There has passed in the world no greater scene of awful sublimity than that which transpired on Mount Sinai, on the occasion of the promulgation of the Law. Nor can there be arranged words expressive of that scene, more beautiful and impressive than those that accompanied its delivery.

The Law is divided into two tables: the first contains the four first; the second, the six last commandments. The first table teaches the entire system of theology necessary to be understood and believed: the second teaches a complete system of ethics, or moral duties. The system of theological principles and moral duties taught by the Law, allowed of no conjectural rules of interpretation; for all principles necessary to be understood, and all duties required to be performed by it, were to be understood and performed just as they were prescribed – this obligation was *imperious*.

If there could be any distinction made in the obligations of the two tables (which we by no means allow), the greater would seem to be in the observance of the first. So high was God's regard for *slaves*, that they find in the last article of the first table, a protection against hard masters: "Remember the sabbath day to keep it holy – six days shalt thou labor, and do all thy work: but the seventh day is the sabbath of the Lord thy God; in it thou shalt not do any work; thou, nor thy son, nor thy daughter, *nor thy man-servant, nor thy maid-servant,* nor thy cattle, nor thy stranger that is within thy gates: for in six days the Lord made heaven and earth, the sea, and all that in them is, and rested the seventh day; wherefore, the Lord blessed the sabbath day and hallowed it."

Josephus says: "The seventh day we set apart from labor; it is dedicated to the learning of our customs and laws: we think it proper to reflect on them, as well as on any [good] thing else, in order to our avoiding of sin." So great was the veneration of the Hebrews for the sabbath, that under the most pressing emergency, they refused to do what they supposed would be a violation of its sanctity. Speaking of Mattathias and his followers (who, when required by Antiochus to offer sacrifices which they considered unlawful, disobeyed, and had taken shelter from his indignation in caves of the desert), our author says: "They, the soldiers of Antiochus, burnt them as they were in the caves, without resistance, and without as much as stopping up the entrances of the caves. And they avoided to defend themselves on that day because they were not willing to break in upon the honor they owed the sabbath, even in such distresses; for our law requires that we rest upon that day."

The stringency of the rule, as observed by the Hebrews, was relaxed by our Saviour: acts of necessity and mercy may be performed on the Sabbath day, without violating its holiness; so we are taught in the following Scripture: "And he was teaching in one of the synagogues on the sabbath. And, behold there was a woman which had a spirit of infirmity eighteen years, and was bowed together, and could in no wise lift up herself. And when Jesus saw her, he called her to Him, and said unto her, Woman, thou art loosed from thine infirmity: and He laid His hand on her, and immediately she was made straight, and glorified God. And the ruler of the synagogue answered with indignation, because that Jesus had healed on the sabbath day, and said unto the people, There are six days in which men ought to work; in them, therefore, come and be healed, and not on the sabbath day. The Lord then answered him, and said, Thou hypocrite! doth not each one of you, on the sabbath, loose his ox or his ass from the stall, and lead him away to watering? And ought not this woman, being a daughter of Abraham, whom Satan hath bound, lo these eighteen years, be loosed from this bond on the sabbath day? And when he had said these things, all His adversaries were ashamed; and all the people rejoiced for all the glorious things that were done by Him:" therefore slaves may, on the sabbath day, be lawfully employed in acts of *necessity* and *mercy*.

Section 2

That the Hebrew people, and their proselytes, formed the Church of God until after the resurrection of our Lord Jesus Christ, is a fact in which all orthodox Christians agree. The Hebrew people, the Church, had every rule which their system required, prescribed to them, relative to slaves. After our Saviour came, and subsequently, when religion was to be offered to the Gentiles, as such, alterations in the rules relative to slaves, became necessary and were made.

One of the most remarkable features, in the altered system, was the recognition of unbelieving masters, or masters not of the

Church, that is, unprofessing Gentile masters. Christian servants are required to yield obedience, as readily to unbelieving as to believing masters; and the requirements of the new rules are as binding upon unbelieving, as they are upon believing masters.

It is matter of admiration to contemplate the precision with which the slavery of the United States adjusts itself to the requirements of the Bible system. Now, it is the Bible system of slavery that we advocate, and not any system, or course, outside of that system. Any system of slavery outside of the Bible system, we regard as of human origin, and therefore an abuse.

But it may be said that there are masters who do not regard the requirements of the Bible in the premises; allowing that there are, we remark, that such disregard amounts to abuse of the system; and we further remark, that every act of abuse is an exception to the rule, and not the rule itself, which is that of general, if not universal obedience. If this objection be still urged, we ask, What is it that men have not abused? Who is prepared to answer that question? No system should be condemned for the abuses connected with it.

Duty of slaves to their masters. – 1. "Servants, be obedient to them that are your masters, according to the flesh, with fear and trembling, in singleness of your heart, as unto Christ; not with eye-service, as men-pleasers; but as the servants of Christ, doing the will of God from the heart; with good will, doing service as to the Lord, and not to men; knowing that whatsoever good thing any man doeth, the same shall he receive of the Lord, whether he be bond or free.

2. "Servants, obey in all things your masters, according to the flesh; not with eye-service, as men-pleasers; but in singleness of heart, fearing God; and whatsoever ye do, do it heartily, as to the Lord, and not unto men; knowing that of the Lord ye shall receive the reward of the inheritance; for ye serve the Lord Christ. But he that doeth wrong shall receive for the wrong which he hath done: and there is no respect of persons.

3. "Exhort servants to be obedient unto their own masters, and to please them well in all things; not answering again; not pur-

loining, but showing all good fidelity: that they may adorn the doctrine of God our Saviour in all things.

4. "Servants, be subject to your masters with all fear; not only to the good and gentle, but also to the froward: for this is thank-worthy, if a man for conscience toward God endure grief, suffering wrongfully: for what is it, if, when ye be buffetted for your faults, ye shall take it patiently? but if when ye do well, and suffer for it, ye take it patiently, this is acceptable with God."

So unmistakably are the duties of servants stated in the above Scriptures, that comment is rendered entirely unnecessary.

Slaves must be content with their condition; for it does not militate against their service of God. – "Let every man abide in the same calling wherein he was called. Art thou called, being a servant? care not for it: but if thou mayest be made free, use it rather. For he that is called in the Lord, being a servant, is the Lord's freeman: likewise also, he that is called, being free, is Christ's servant. Ye are bought with a price; be not ye the servants of men. Brethren, let every man, wherein he is called, therein abide with God."

Dr. Clarke explains the above Scripture thus: 1. "As both the circumcised and uncircumcised, in Christ have the same advantages, and to their believing, the same facilities; so any situation of life is equally friendly to the salvation of the soul, if a man be faithful to the grace he has received. Therefore, in all situations, a Christian should be content; for all things work together for good to him who loves God.

2. "Art thou converted to Christ, while thou art a slave? the property of another person, and bought with his money: care not for it: this will not injure thy Christian condition: but if thou canst obtain thy liberty [and preserve thy Christian character], use it rather; prefer this state for the sake of freedom, and the temporal advantages connected with it.

3. "The man who, being a slave, is converted to the Christian faith, is the Lord's freeman; his condition as a slave does not vitiate any of the privileges to which he is entitled as a Christian: on the other hand, all freemen who receive the grace of Christ,

must consider themselves slaves of the Lord, i.e., His real property, to be employed and disposed of, according to His godly wisdom; who, notwithstanding his state of subjection, will find the service of his master to be perfect freedom.

4. "As truly as your bodies have become the property of your masters, in consequence of his paying down a price for you; so sure you are now the Lord's property, in consequence of your being purchased by the blood of Christ.

"In this Scripture the apostle shows that the Christian religion does not abolish our civil connections: – in reference to them, where it finds us, there it leaves us. In whatever relation we stood before our embracing Christianity, there we stand still; our secular condition being no farther changed, than as it may be affected by the melioration of our moral character."

Duty of masters to their slaves. – "And ye masters do the same things unto them [see Eph. 6], forbearing threatening; knowing that your Master also, is in heaven; neither is there respect of persons with Him.

"Masters give unto your servants that which is just and equal; knowing that ye also, have a Master in heaven."

Relation in which Christianity regards master and slave. – "Let as many servants as are under the yoke, count their own masters worthy of all honor, that the name of God and His doctrine, be not blasphemed.

"And they that have believing masters, let them not despise them, because they are brethren; but rather do them service, because they are faithful and beloved, par takers of the benefit."

False teachers rebuked. – "If any man teach otherwise, and consent not to wholesome words, even the words of our Lord Jesus Christ, and the doctrine which is according to godliness, he is proud, knowing nothing, but doating about questions and strifes of words, whereof cometh envy, strife, railings, evil surmisings, perverse disputings of men of corrupt minds, and destitute of the truth, supposing that gain is godliness: from such withdraw thyself." How particularly and distinctly is the character of the modern abolitionist drawn by the apostle!

It is easy to perceive here, that it is the intention of the apostle to protect the relation of master and slave, from the assaults of mischievous intermeddlers. How distinct is the apostle in all this! if he had written to-day, he could not have been more explicit. Will those to whom the rebuke applies, be admonished by it? Most likely, they will not.

Section 8

Fugitive slaves. – The American Union is formed by the confederation of several independent, sovereign nations – States. In the internal organizations of these States, are found institutions peculiar to each. Things exist in one which have no existence in another. This state of things necessarily creates a comity between the States thus united. This comity requires that each State should recognize and sustain the internal organization of all and of each: without this, harmony cannot exist, and without harmony it is impossible to preserve union; therefore, we assert, that the destruction of the comity of the States will result in the destruction of the union of the States.

The union of the States is declared and maintained by a common Constitution. By this Constitution the individual States have agreed to suspend the exercise of certain well-defined powers, for certain well-defined purposes. No powers but those expressly granted (and of course, those that are incidental), can be exercised by the common government. The granted powers relate to but few objects of State authority (and that from necessity); amongst these few objects, however, is that of slavery; with which the common government has but a very limited connection.

It does not fall within the range of our undertaking, to discuss the principles here stated; that may be the duty of the political economist, not ours: be that as it may, the object we have in introducing these statements, is to show the extent of the connection of the common government with the subject now to be investigated.

Although the African slave trade had been prohibited by

the Congress of 1776, it was in operation at the time of the adoption of the common Constitution. By that instrument it is declared, "The migration or importation of such persons as any of the States now existing shall think proper to admit, shall not be prohibited by the Congress, prior to the year 1808; but a tax or duty may be imposed on such importation, not exceeding ten dollars for each person." Congress, in March, 1807, passed an act, declaring the trade at an end on the 1st day of January, 1808.

A further provision of the Constitution, is, "No person held to service or labor in one State, under the laws thereof, escaping into another, shall in consequence of any law or regulation therein, be discharged from such service or labor, but shall be delivered up on claim of the party to whom such service or labor may be due." These two provisions of the Constitution contain all the connection the common government has with the institution of slavery (having legislated on both subjects, the power of Congress is therefore exhausted). Pursuant to the last provision of the Constitution, Congress passed acts for the return to their owners, of fugitive slaves. That it is the duty of every good citizen to assist in the execution of these laws, and that none but unworthy citizens will oppose their execution, it is useless for us to remark.

No constitutional laws have been more violently assailed and obstructed, than the fugitive-slave laws, by abolitionists: they have been taught to believe that the following Scripture, "Thou shalt not deliver unto his master, the servant which is escaped from his master unto thee: he shall dwell with thee, even among you, in that place which he shall choose in one of thy gates, where it liketh him best: thou shalt not oppress him;" authorizes, nay more, requires, that they should not deliver up fugitive slaves. A greater perversion of sacred truth, perhaps, was never committed.

The twenty-third chapter of Deuteronomy, in which the above Scripture is found, shows that Moses was giving to the Israelites instructions respecting certain nations of people; some of whom were never to enter "the congregation of the Lord;" that is, the Church; others were not to enter the congregation until the "third generation."

This was the punishment inflicted upon these nations for causes mentioned in the chapter. Now, the above Scripture alludes to the slaves of these peoples. If a slave desired to abandon idolatry and to embrace the religion of the Israelites, and with this view, escaped from his master, then he was not to be given up, but to be protected. In this arrangement, we see the divine goodness manifested in favor of the slaves of masters, who could not themselves become members of the Hebrew Church. The slave, who was not to blame for the idolatry of his master, has a way provided for him, whereby his salvation may be secured. This is the obvious meaning of the text. Dr. Clarke says: "In any other case, it would have been injustice to have harbored the runaway."

And now for the application. How is it with abolitionists; do slaves of idolatrous masters seek among them to embrace the true faith? Verily, we conceive that their teachings are much worse than any species of idolatry! When they succeed in getting a slave to escape from his master, is it their practice or their purpose, to place him under correct religious training? Nay, they abandon the poor fugitive, and thereby cause him, in too many instances, to renounce the religion in which he has been educated, and which, perhaps, he professed; thus carrying him back, if not to idolatry, to at least as hopeless a condition as that would be.

The Bible regulated the subject, now under consideration, as long ago as A. M. 2093. On Abraham's first visit to Egypt, he procured for Sarah a maid-slave named Hagar. Sarah, after their return from Egypt, continuing childless, said to Abraham (who was then called Abram), "Behold now, the Lord hath restrained me from bearing: I pray thee, go in unto my maid; it may be that I may obtain children by her. And Abram hearkened to the voice of Sarai. And Sarai, Abram's wife, took Hagar her maid, the Egyptian, after Abram had dwelt ten years in the land of Canaan, and gave her to her husband Abram, to be his wife. And he went in unto Hagar, and she conceived: and when she saw that she had conceived, her mistress was despised in her eyes. And Sarai said unto Abram, My wrong be upon thee: I have given my maid into thy bosom; and when she saw that she had conceived, I was despised in her eyes: the Lord judge between me and thee. But Abram said unto Sarai, Behold, thy maid is in thy hand; do to her as it pleaseth thee. And when Sarai dealt hardly with her, she fled from her face.

"And the angel of the Lord found her by a fountain of water in the wilderness, by the fountain in the way to Shur. And he said, Hagar, Sarai's maid, whence camest thou? and whither wilt thou go? And she said, I flee from the face of my mistress Sarai. And the angel of the Lord said unto her. Return to thy mistress, and submit thyself under her hands.

"And the angel of the Lord said unto her. Behold, thou art with child, and shalt bear a son, and shalt call his name Ishmael; because the Lord hath heard thy affliction. And he will be a wild man; his hand will be against every man, and every man's hand against him: and he shall dwell in the presence of all his brethren."

This Scripture settles the facts, that Hagar was a slave; that she was, by her mistress, treated hardly; that she ran away; that the angel of the Lord ordered her back to her mistress, and commanded her to submit herself under her hands. These facts are stated so explicitly and unmistakably, that the propriety of remarking upon them is, at least, questionable; and were it not that the application of the case to slavery in the United States, might be overlooked, we certainly should be silent.

The angel commanded Hagar to return to her mistress, and accompanies the command with the assurance that her posterity should be numerous and independent. This announcement received its accomplishment, literally and fully, as the history of the Bedouins and wandering Arabs testifies.

So with the slavery of the United States. The objects proposed, perhaps we had better write purposed, to be accomplished by it, are:

1. The training of the slave, for his personal benefit and advantage.

2. The redemption of Africa from all her woes, and making her an independent Christian nation.

Now, individual slaves escaping from their owners, will not

defeat the accomplishment of the purpose; at most, it can but delay it; but it is the removal, to some extent, of the agency through which the purposes are to be accomplished. It is easy, therefore, to see, that persons assisting slaves to escape from their owners, or refusing to deliver to their owners fugitive slaves, are "fighting against God."

The duty imposed by the above Scripture, is exceedingly plain; it is to follow the example of the angel – see that the fugitive returns to his master.

But, there may be those that will not feel satisfied that the foregoing Scripture is sufficient to establish the fact for which it is adduced. Without entering into the argument of the question thus started, in favor of our position, we produce below Scripture that is not liable to any objection whatever, and which is decisive of the question: – *St. Paul's Epistle to Philemon, is devoted exclusively to this subject – it has but the one object:* the reader is referred to the Epistle.

This Epistle was written A.D, 62. Some authors of distinction have thought it strange, that a private letter to a friend, on a subject not connected with the ordinary business of an apostle, should have been written under inspiration, and found its way into the Sacred Canon. It is part of the arrangement God has made, connected with the objects of slavery – when considered in this connection, it is no matter of surprise at all. Dr. Clarke deduces the following conclusions from the Epistle, which we adopt with some alterations:

1. In a religious point of view, all genuine Christian converts are on a level: Onesimus, the slave, on his conversion, becomes the apostle's beloved son, and Philemon's brother.

2. Christianity makes no change in men's civil affairs: even a slave does not become a freeman by Christian baptism – he must still serve his master.

3. No slave should be either taken or retained from his master, without the master's consent.

4. We should do good unto all men, and not be above helping the meanest slave when we have the opportunity.

5. Restitution is due where an injury has been done, unless the injured party freely forgive.

6. The ministers of the Gospel should learn to know the worth of an immortal soul, and be as ready to use their talents for the conversion of slaves, as the great and opulent; and prize the converted slave as highly as the converted master; showing no sinful respect of persons.

7. Christianity properly understood, and its doctrines properly applied, becomes the most powerful means of the melioration of men; the wicked and profligate, when brought under its influence, become useful members of society. It can transform a worthless slave into a pious, amiable and useful man; and make him, not only happier and better in himself, but also, a blessing to others.

CHAPTER THREE
Importation of Slaves Into the United States

Section 1

How distinctly did every feature of every phase of slavery pass in review before him, when the prophet wrote the following prophecy. The condition of the slave in Africa; on board the transport ship; in the hands of the importer, and in America, are alluded to with unmistakable precision: "Thus saith the Lord, The labor of Egypt, *and merchandise of Ethiopia,* and of the Sabeans, men of stature, *shall come over unto thee, and they shall be thine:* they shall *come after thee;* in *chains they shall come over,* and they shall fall down unto thee; they shall make supplication unto thee, saying, *Surely God is in thee,* and there is none else; *there is no God."* Commentators have given no special application to this prophecy. The use we make of it, is in no way inconsistent with what they say about it; all of them speak of it cautiously. One of them, Lowth, says: "This seems to relate to the future admission of the Gentiles into the Church of God. And, perhaps, these particular nations may be named, by a metonomy common in all poetry, for powerful and wealthy nations in general." We here give the prophecy its special application and meaning, we conceive.

African slavery in the United States is to be regarded as a blessing, chiefly to the slave himself. The African was not reduced to slavery by being brought to the United States – no injustice, in this respect, has been done him, by bringing him here – he was a slave in his own country (slavery is an African not an American institution) – subject to a much more severe bondage there, as we have shown, than it is possible for him ever to experience here – it was a great melioration of his condition to bring him here: suppose he had been left in his own country, in the hands of his African master, who does not see, who will not admit that his condition would have been much worse than it is possible for his condition to be in his present situation. But when, in addition to the immediate advantages realized by the slave, in the change of position, we consider his further improvement, and the ultimate elevation of his race, we cannot fail to admit the great good which is to result from slavery; every heart touched with the least gratitude, should be thankful for an institution that is to produce such results.

But when our attention is directed to the conduct of the importer, then it is that we may indulge a just indignation: the slave in his hands, was regarded merely as merchandise – "the merchandise of Ethiopia." Every feeling of humanity is outraged, in view of the cruelties practiced by the importer; who always will, to the last, receive, as he deserves, the denunciations of the good.

The Pope's authority to dispose of infidel nations, or those he was pleased to regard as such, grew out of the crusades. According to this doctrine, Christian princes "had the right to invade, ravage and seize upon the territories of all infidel nations, under the plea of defeating the enemies of Christ, and extending the sway of His holy Church on earth." The infidels themselves were left at the disposal of their conquerers.

In conformity with the established doctrine, John I., of Portugal, invaded Northern Africa and established his standard at Cueta. Here his enterprising son, Henry, conceived the idea of passing to India by circumnavigating Africa. This idea was a long time maturing; its practical demonstration, however, was at length entered upon. The first attempts resulted in the exploration of the western coasts of Africa, as far south as Cape de Verde and Azore

Islands. Without accomplishing his undertaking, Henry died in 1473: his death delayed this enterprise until 1487, when Vasco de Gama, a veteran navigator in the employment of the Portuguese government, doubled the Cape of Good Hope. Thus was the door of the African slave-trade thrown open, into which the nations and peoples of Christendom impetuously rushed.

As we are about to enter upon some general details of this trade, it may not be out of place here, to state the recognized divisions into which the peoples of Africa are thrown. There are seven ascertainable varieties, to wit: 1. Hottentot. 2. Kaffir. 3. Abyssinian. 4. Egyptian. 5. Numidian. 6. Nubian. 7. Negro. The Negro (Cushite), who retains his physical identity in all climates and under all circumstances, is found scattered amongst all the other varieties – a slave.

Section 2

Columbus discovered the New World in 1492. The first permanent settlement attempted, as is well known, was on the island of St. Domingo. In 1497, a dangerous conspiracy, headed by Francisco Roldan, broke out on the island, which continued for two years, when it was adjusted by Columbus assigning lands and Indian slaves to the conspirators. This arrangement resulted, says Irving, in the "repartimientos, or distribution of free Indians among the colonists, afterwards generally adopted and shamefully abused, throughout the Spanish colonies." Attempts have been made to relieve the course pursued by Columbus of its injustice, by assimilating it to the feudal system of Europe, the Indians being the slaves of the system. It must be said, and this affords the best apology for Columbus, in justice to the admiral, that the scheme did not originate with him, and that he yielded to it with reluctance almost amounting to compulsion. This arrangement stipulated that the Indian chiefs, called caciques, should furnish each Spaniard with a certain number of people, for the purpose of cultivating their grounds: the terms were soon applied to working in mines. Again does justice to Columbus require it to be stated, that this was done under the administration of Bobadilla. Ovando, who super-seded Bobadilla in the government of the island, extended this measure to the utmost limit of cruelty. Some idea of the sufferings of the Indians, by the oppressions inflicted upon them, may be derived from the statement, that in less time than twelve years from the settlement of the Island, "several hundred thousand of its native inhabitants had perished; miserable victims to the grasping avarice of white men," calling themselves Christians!

Ovando was sent out in 1502. The instructions under which he was to act, drawn up the year before, show great solici-tude on the part of the sovereigns, particularly of Isabella, whose benevolent heart was always full of sympathy for the oppressed, in favor of the Indians. Alluding to these instructions, Irving says: "But while the sovereigns were making regulations for the relief of the Indians; with that inconsistency frequent in human judg-ment, they encouraged a gross invasion of the rights and welfare of another race of human beings. Among their various decrees, on the occasion, we find the first trace of negro slavery in the New World. It was permitted to carry to the colonies, negro slaves born among Christians; that is to say, slaves born in Seville and other parts of Spain; the children and descendants of natives brought from the Atlantic coast of Africa, with which a traffic of the kind had for some time been carried on, by the Spaniards and Portu-guese." The license given was so eagerly seized upon, that in 1503, only two years after its grant, the merciless Ovando re-quested that the number of Negroes on the island might not be increased by importation.

Thus was Negro slavery introduced into the New World: the following facts will show how it advanced at this time. We are indebted to Irving for dates and other facts. In 1510, king Ferdinand ordered African slaves to be employed in the mines (the mines having become attached to the crown; previously they had been the property of private persons, and Negroes had been em-ployed in them). In 1511, the king ordered that a great number of slaves should be procured from Guinea, and carried to the island. In 1512 and 1513, he repeated his orders. In 1516, Charles V., successor of Ferdinand, granted licenses to the Flemings, to import Negroes into the colonies. This license was received with eagerness by those in whose favor it was made, and an extensive importation ensued.

There is a singular fact connected with the good Las Casas, missionary to the Indians on St. Domingo, which we here notice. His sensibilities were easily moved in favor of the Indians – no efforts were left untried on his part to serve them – but he had no sympathies for the Negroes. He participated in the popular opinions, that one Negro could perform without inconvenience to himself, the labor of four Indians – that the Africans were not affected by their transportation to the New World – that they were slaves in their own country – that they thrived in the New World as well, if not better, than they did in Guinea – that slavery was the natural condition of the African! We cannot but perceive and admire the workings of Providence in all this.

Section 3

The other nations of Europe were decidedly against regarding the claim of Spain to the territory of the New World, as conclusive; either on the ground of her having led the way to it, or of the Pope's grant. They contended that Spain had no right to any other territory than that actually visited by her fleets, or occupied by her people. As respects territory falling within the limits of the United States, this assumption confined Spain to the Floridas, and even that she was not allowed, very quietly, to retain.

In 1496, John Cabot and his son Sebastian, by private enterprise, but with the approbation, and under the auspices of the English Government, sailed on a voyage of discovery. In 1497, they discovered the American continent, in the latitude of fifty-six degrees, as is supposed – thence they returned to England.

In 1498, Sebastian Cabot reached the continent in the latitude of fifty-eight degrees. He then turned south, and proceeded along the coast to a point near the southern boundary of Maryland: thence he returned to England. The proceedings of the Cabots, formed the claim that England set up to the northern Atlantic portion of the United States. A claim which, perhaps, she was more successful in maintaining, than just in proposing.

It was not until 1504, that France entered into the business of discovery in the New World. However, the Newfoundland fisheries soon rewarded her enterprise. The Gulf of St. Lawrence was examined, and some further discoveries were made on the coast. Francis I., then occupying the throne of France, encouraged the colonization of the newly-discovered territories. The French, under the lead of their priests, soon found their way up the river St. Lawrence, to the Lakes; from the Lakes across to the Mississippi, and down that river to the Gulf of Mexico: forming military and trading posts at short distances from each other; thus they girded inland the English and Spanish discoveries.

In 1524, Verrazani, a Florentine, in the service of France, passed along much of the American coast which had been traversed by the Cabots; as far south as Wilmington, in North Carolina, perhaps as far, in that direction, as Tybee, in Georgia. A dispute arose between England and France, relative to the right of each, respecting the discoveries: this dispute was finally adjusted by the treaty of Utrecht; France relinquishing to England her claim.

In 1609, Hudson, in the employment of the Dutch East India Company, sailed in search of the north-western passage. Becoming impeded by ice, he turned down the American coast, and on the third day of September, anchored within Sandy Hook. After a short delay, he passed through the Narrows and anchored in the beautiful Bay at the mouth of the North River. He proceeded up the river to a point above the city of Hudson, and dispatched a boat which ascended the river above Albany. The region thus explored, took the name of New Netherlands. The interests involved were transferred by the East to the Dutch West India Company. A dispute arose between England and the Dutch about New Netherlands, which, of course, was settled in favor of England. When was England known to relinquish a claim to territory, however unwarrantable the pretext upon which it was founded?

The transfer of New Netherlands, placed in the hands of England the entire territory composing the old thirteen States.

Section 4

Properly to understand the heinousness of the crimes of those who engaged in the importation of Africans into the New World, it must be borne in mind that there were two classes in Africa, to wit, master and slave: this distinction the importers were unwilling to allow; they wished to regard all alike – master and slave, as free game. As an illustration of this, we produce the following statement: a titled subject of Great Britain, Sir John Hawkins, who engaged in the importation, at an early period, says, his manner of proceeding was to fire the towns and seize the inhabitants as they were attempting to escape the flames. At one town, containing eight thousand inhabitants, he succeeded in capturing two hundred and fifty persons, whom he sold as slaves. The triumphant manner in which Hawkins relates the success of his mode of proceeding, and such conduct passing without censure or rebuke from any quarter, manifests the depravity of the times.

This Hawkins, in 1562, brought a cargo of Africans to St. Domingo, and either bartered them for, or bought with their purchase-price, the rich products of the island, which were of great value in England. This excited both the attention and the cupidity of Queen Elizabeth, who immediately engaged in the business as a co-adventurer. But Hawkins alone is not to be held up as the only kidnapper; the other traders pursued similar plans for their supply of slaves: the only difference is this. Sir John very imprudently boasted of his deeds; others very prudently concealed theirs. So, it is the duty of impartial history to state the facts.

The African slave-trade continued, principally, to be an object of private enterprise until 1713, when, by the treaty of Utrecht, it became systematized in the hands of England. By this treaty "Her Britannic Majesty did offer and undertake, by persons whom she shall appoint, to bring into the West Indies of America, belonging to His Catholic Majesty, in the space of thirty years,

ONE HUNDRED AND FORTY-FOUR THOUSAND NE-
GROES, at the rate of four thousand eight hundred, in each of the
said thirty years." Her Britannic Majesty might import as many
more as she thought proper, or her means would allow, but she
was not to fall below the stipulated number. No Frenchman, nor
Spaniard, nor any one else, might import into the Spanish-Ameri-
can dependencies, one Negro. Her Britannic Majesty took good
care also, to protect her own American possessions from the intru-
sion of other slave-traders. *Thus the African slave-trade in America became a royal monopoly.* Queen Anne boasted, in her speech
to Parliament, of the success of her plan, in thus obtaining for
English subjects a new slave-market in the Spanish "West Indies."
The Queen admitted, as a co-partner in this business (for what
equivalent is not stated), Philip V., of Spain, who took one-fourth
of the common stock: she reserved to herself one-fourth, and permitted her subjects to divide the remaining half among themselves.
Here we have the record of the strange fact, that the Queen of
England bargained to the King of Spain, the right to impart Negroes into his own colonies!

Section 5

The transport-ship, called Guineaman, was generally some
old East India, or whaling ship, whose capacious depth of hold
was fitted up with slave-decks, upon which were arranged, in
regular order, cargoes consisting of from five to eight hundred, or
a thousand or more, slaves: they were conveyed in canoes from
the shore to the ship, where they were reduced to a state of nu-
dity; except in some instances, when a slight covering was placed
about the loins: their heads were closely shaved – they were organized into messes of from ten to fifteen individuals; after eating, a
bucket of salt-water was furnished each mess, for the purpose of
washing hands – a guard was placed over each mess, at meal-time,
for the purpose of detecting those who refused to eat, for they
often resolved on starvation; when this was observed, the "cat"
generally brought the refractory to a proper course: their allow-

ance of water was generally about a quart in twenty-four hours: as often as three times a week their mouths were rinsed with vinegar, and a small quantity of rum was allowed each slave, every morning: the sexes were invariably kept apart, during the voyage: the men were shaved, without soap, once a week. These precautions, and many others, were deemed necessary to the health of the slaves, during the passage: notwithstanding, contagious disorders would frequently break out among them, by which cargoes have been reduced one-half, sometimes more. In such cases, a fatal dose would be administered to those first attacked, in order that by their removal, the others might be preserved! This was done under the plea of necessity and humanity!

[The contraband trade has brought into use a description of craft called clipper. These vessels vary from forty to one hundred and fifty tons, and are, generally, of schooner rig. They proceed to Africa, and hover about the coast until an opportunity occurs, when they slip into some river, or creek, and become concealed among the trees which grow upon its margin. Here, from some neighboring barracoon, they procure their cargoes. It is almost impossible to conceive how one of these vessels of only one hundred tons, can stow away three hundred and fifty slaves; means, however, are found to do it. They compel them to lie down in each other's laps; between decks affording but twenty-two inches space! We have the recorded instance, of *seven hundred and forty-nine slaves* being packed in the hold of a vessel of *one hundred and sixty-five tons!* This appears to be almost incredible.

Captain Bell, of the United States' Navy, in 1840, writes: "From the best information that could be obtained, there are now, and have been for several years passed, shipped from Africa upwards of two hundred and fifty thousand slaves per annum. This appears incredible to those who have not examined into the subject; but when it is considered that sixty-two vessels, carrying, or prepared to carry, upon an average, three hundred each, were sent into Sierra Leone last year, in addition to those sent to the Cape of Good Hope, and captured in the West Indies, and on the coast of Brazil; and that not more than one in six is captured, as I was credibly informed, it will be found to fall within the above estimate. In consequence of the chance of capture, the poor Negroes suffer ten-fold more misery than in the early stages of the traffic; they crowd them in small, fast-sailing vessels, at the rate of two, and sometimes even four to the ton, with a slave-deck but two feet two inches high; as was the case with a slaver lately sent into Sierra Leone. So dreadful is their situation, that one in ten dies in crossing the ocean; consequently, twenty-five thousand human beings are thus destroyed in a year!"

It is a matter of some importance to know how, if so many slaves are lost in their transportation, the persons engaged in this business realize any profit from it; the case is susceptible of easy explanation: the average price of slaves at the barracoon, is forty dollars, in goods; the average price on Cuba, is four hundred dollars, in cash. This statement, also, enables us to perceive how it is, that men continue to hazard the risks connected with the illicit traffic – the probable profit forms the inducement.]

Section 6

Of the stowing away of the slaves, in the Guineaman, Foote says: "The slaves were obliged to lie on their backs, and were shackled by their ankles; the left one being fettered close to the right of the next: so that the whole number in one line, formed a single, living chain. When one died, the body remained, during the night, or during bad weather, secured to the two between whom he was. The height between decks was so little, that a man of ordinary size could hardly sit upright. During good weather, a gang of slaves was taken on the spar-deck, and there remained for a short time. In bad weather, when the hatches were closed, death from suffocation would necessarily occur. It can, therefore, be easily understood, that the athletic strangled the weaker intentionally, in order to procure more space; and that, when striving to get near some aperture affording air to breathe, many would be injured, or killed, in the struggle."

In 1792, the British House of Commons collected some evidence relative to the enormities of the slave-trade; from this collection Foote makes the following extracts: James Morley, gunner of the Medway, states, "He has seen them under great difficulty of breathing; the women, particularly, often got upon the beams, where the gratings are often raised with banisters, about four feet above the combings, to give air, but they are generally driven down, because they take the air from the rest. He had known rice held in the mouths of sea-sick slaves, until they were almost strangled. He has seen the surgeon's mate force the panniken between their teeth, and throw the medicine over them, so that not half of it went into their mouths – the poor wretches wallowing in their blood, hardly having life, and this with blows of the cat."

Dr. Thomas Trotter, surgeon of the Brooks, says, "He has seen the slaves drawing their breath with all those laborious and anxious efforts for life which are observed in expiring animals, subjected by experiment to foul air, or in the exhausted receiver of an air-pump. Has also seen them when the tarpaulins have inadvertently been thrown over the gratings, attempting to heave them up, crying out, 'kickeraboo! kickeraboo!' i.e., *we are dying!* On removing the tarpaulin and gratings, they would fly to the hatchways, with all the signs of terror and dread of suffocation. Many whom he has seen in a dying state, have recovered by being brought on the deck: others were irrecoverably lost by suffocation, having had no previous signs of indisposition."

With regard to the Garland's voyage (a slaver, in 1788), the testimony is, "Some of the diseased were obliged to be kept on deck. The slaves, both when ill and well, were frequently forced to eat against their inclinations; were whipped with a cat, if they refused. The parts on which their shackles are fastened, are often excoriated by the violent exercise they are forced to take, and of this they made many grievous complaints to him (deponent). Fell in with the Hero, Wilson, which had lost, deponent thinks, three hundred and sixty slaves, by death; he is certain, more than half her cargo; learnt this from the surgeon; they had died mostly of the small-pox. Surgeon also told him, that when removed from one place to another, they left marks of their skin and blood upon the deck, and that it was the most horrid sight he had ever seen." These statements bring us in view of some of the horrors of the "middle passage;" an expression of darkest portent.

It is no matter of surprise that the sailor (disposed to be superstitious), in the silence of nightly vigils, imagines, as he navigates the dark waters of Africa's coast, that he sees on each wave-top the troubled ghost of some child of oppression. No wonder, that when the storm presses hard upon his bark, he sees the phantom slave-ship as she scuds by, and hears from her captives the shrieks of despair. No marvel, when he knows that on the bottom beneath him, in confusion, lie countless heaps of the skeletons of the victims of cruelty, he breathes hard and anxiously; and no wonder that his anxiety is relieved, and his breathing freer, when he passes the precincts of the haunted district.

Section 7

There are no sources of information in which implicit confidence can be placed, whereby it may be ascertained how many African slaves were imported into the New World; that fact must ever remain unascertained: conjectures will continue to be made, but history never will record the undisputed fact. Bancroft says: "Raynal considers the number of Negroes exported by all European nations from Africa before 1776, to have been NINE MILLIONS; and the considerate German historian of the slave-trade, Albert Hüne, deems his statement too small."

After assigning his reasons for his opinion, Bancroft says: "We shall not err very much, if, for the century previous to the prohibition of the slave-trade by the American Congress, in 1776, we assume the number imported by the English, into the Spanish, French and English West Indies, as well as the English continental colonies, to have been collectively nearly THREE MILLIONS; to which are to be added more than a quarter of a million purchased in Africa, and thrown into the Atlantic, on the passage."

There are some other facts belonging to this connection which do not partake of the uncertainty of which we had to speak in the above paragraph. We allude to the American importers: their names, residences, and the extent to which they were engaged in this business, may be ascertained with exactness; nothing is required for the purpose of making these developments but a little patient research. And it is possible, nay more, it is probable, it will be ascertained that some of our Northern fellow-citizens, who at this day are loudest and longest in their denunciations of slavery and slave-holders, are the descendants of importers, inheriting, if not always their names, at least the fortunes they acquired in this business. Really, we do not see how the progeny could be other than it is, when the ancestry was of such a type.

The slave-trade in the New World extended over a period of three hundred and seven years; that is to say, from the year 1501, when it commenced by the importation of Negro slaves into St. Domingo, to the year 1808, when it was finally closed by the Federal Constitution. From this period, however, must be deducted the short time that the trade was suspended by the Congress of 1776.

England was engaged in the trade two hundred and forty-six years; that is to say, from the year 1562, when Elizabeth became the co-partner of Hawkins, to the year 1808. This period includes the reigns of Elizabeth, of James I., of Charles I., the period of the Commonwealth, or Cromwell's administration, of Charles II., of James II., of William III., of Anne, of George I., of George II., and of George III. England amassed large sums from the slave-trade. Bancroft asserts that "she gained by the sale of the children of Africa into bondage in America, the capital which built up and confirmed the British empire in Hindostan."

There is no subject purely human connected with the world's history, that presents to the mind such an amount of unmitigated horror as attaches to the importers of African slaves. The excesses committed by them outrage every principle of humanity, every feeling of benevolence. This, no doubt, accounts for the fact, that the historians of England pass over the subject with but imperfect allusions to it. This will not do; it is not fair. A source from which the government derived such large revenues for so long a time, requires that its *minutiæ* should be written without regard to the injustice connected with it. The chapter (the blackest in England's history) that is to relate these horrible details, remains to be written; to the writer of that chapter we commend a paragraph written by Mr. Jefferson, to be found in Tucker. This paragraph was in the draft of the Declaration of Independence, presented by that wise statesman to the convention of 1776, and by the convention stricken out, because they supposed the language used too strong at that time: "He – the king – has waged cruel war against human nature itself, violating its most sacred rights of life and liberty in the persons of a distant people who never offended him, captivating and carrying them into slavery in another hemisphere, or to incur miserable death in their transportation thither. This piratical warfare, the opprobrium of infidel nations, is the warfare of the Christian king of Great Britain. Determined to keep open a market where men should be bought and sold, he had prostituted his negative for suppressing every legislative attempt to prohibit or to restrain this execrable commerce. And that this assemblage of horrors might want no fact of distinguished dye, he is now exciting those very people to rise in arms among us, and to purchase that liberty of which he has deprived them, by murdering the people on whom he also obtruded them; thus paying off former crimes committed against the liberties of one people with crimes which he urges them to commit against the lives of another." Without this paragraph, or the substance of it, that chapter will be incomplete.

Section 8

While European nations and monarchs were principally engaged in the importation of African slaves into the New World, it is proper to remark, that the peoples of the American Colonies, afterwards States, more particularly those of the Middle and New England States, became largely involved in it before it was prohibited by law. And so lucrative has this trade ever been, that at this day, after it has been abolished nearly half a century, instances are frequent of vessels owned in the Northern section of the Union, engaging in it. It is in vain that the United States, France and England, maintain strong naval forces on the African coasts; the traders find means to elude them, and cargoes of slaves continue to be landed in ports contiguous to the United States. The uncontradicted statement is, that during the past twelve mouths [1855-'56], twenty-one vessels, that is to say, six barks, two brigs, and thirteen schooners, engaged in the African slave-trade, belong to the port of New York, besides others which belong to Philadelphia and Boston.

It is impossible to ascertain with mathematical certainty how many African slaves were imported into the American colonies by the parties engaged in their importation, but it is supposed by those who have undertaken the ascertainment of the fact, that in 1776, when all the colonies possessed slaves, the number was OVER THREE HUNDRED THOUSAND. Some writers go largely over this estimate, which is the lowest.

It is asserted that the first foot-prints made by a Negro slave on that part of the American continent falling within the Union, were made in Virginia soil, in August, 1620. Then a Dutch ship (some say a man-of-war; if so, a public ship) entered James River, having on board twenty African slaves for sale.

Bancroft states that the guilt of "first participating in the slave-trade," was brought upon the American colonies by "one Thomas Keyser and one James Smith," who in 1615 fitted out their ship in Boston, "and sailed for Guinea, to trade for Negroes." [Why not say, "that the first American Colony which engaged in the importation of African slaves, was Massachusetts"? The truth would have been much better told. Some of the colonies, at the time mentioned, had no existence; and amongst those that did exist, there was no political connection whatever. Each colony must be held accountable for its own acts then, as each State must be held accountable for its own acts now. The form of expression adopted by Bancroft involves all the colonies in conduct for which

Massachusetts alone is accountable.] He says, "But throughout Massachusetts the cry of justice was raised against them, as malefactors and murderers. Richard Saltonstall, a worthy assistant, felt himself moved by his duty as a magistrate, to denounce the act of stealing Negroes, as 'expressly contrary to the law of God, and the law of the country.' The guilty men were committed for the offence, and, after advice with the elders, the representatives of the people, bearing 'witness against the heinous crime of man-stealing,' ordered the Negroes to be restored, at the public charge, 'to their native country, with a letter [to whom was this letter written?] expressing the indignation of the general court' at their wrongs." We have high regard for Massachusetts; the patriotism and public spirit of her citizens are not to be questioned, and we appreciate fully the motive of Bancroft; it is in every sense praiseworthy. What a pity it was, however, that Massachusetts bestowed such an amount of sympathy upon Negroes, that when afterwards her own citizens [Quakers and witches], stood in need of it, it was all gone! It is so now. It is said, that at this time there are not many Quakers in Massachusetts, fewer witches, and plenty of abolitionists. Happy State!

The African slave-trade possessed this sensible distinction, legitimate and illegitimate, or legal and illegal. The legitimate trade allowed the purchase of slaves for what their African owner was pleased to regard as a fair price. The illegitimate trade consisted in the kidnapping [stealing, as the Massachusetts authorities very correctly termed it] of any and all, without regard to condition. This involved both master and slave. The illegitimate trade, for obvious reasons, was generally preferred and engaged in by the importers. Whenever it could be, it was practiced. Now, it was the illegitimate trade which the good people of Massachusetts condemned, and which the authorities proceeded to punish. The statement of facts made by Bancroft, does not warrant the conclusion, that had Keyser and Smith been engaged in the legitimate trade, their enterprise would have been interrupted. It was the "man-stealing "that very properly excited the indignation of the people.

Section 9

The abstract question of slavery was never submitted to the peoples of the American Colonies. The institution was forced upon them by England principally, France, Holland and Spain; therefore, the discussion of the question at this time is improper, for it could produce no result whatever. All the interest the people of the South have in slavery, is to ascertain how to manage it.

The year 1620 may be properly regarded as the period that opened the African slave-trade in the colonies. It became so rapid that the colonies were alarmed, and proceeded to arrest it if they might. Virginia passed twenty-three acts in endeavoring to accomplish this object; and so long as the importation was confined to the Dutch, she succeeded in keeping the numbers below what she conceived to be the point of security; but when England undertook the business Virginia was obliged to yield. Mr. Madison, referring to this subject, said, "The British government constantly checked the attempts of Virginia to put a stop to this infernal traffic." Stevens says, "South Carolina soon passed a law prohibiting their further importation. It was rejected by the king in council, who declared the trade 'beneficial and necessary to the mother-country.' Massachusetts, the first State in America which directly participated in the slave-trade, and that, too, through a member of one of the Boston churches, earnestly rebuked the traffic, imposed duties upon Negroes imported, and aimed at other efforts." All this, however, was frustrated by the royal governor, Hutchinson, who pleaded his instructions against it. Stevens continues: "The royal orders to Governor Wentworth directed him not to give his assent to or pass any law imposing duties on Negroes imported into New Hampshire." Without referring farther to the independent action of each colony, their opposition to the importation may be summed up in the words of Bancroft: "The English continental colonies, in the aggregate, were always opposed to the African slave-trade." The importation continued, however, until the Continental Congress in 1776, in accordance with the popular opinion, put a stop to it by enacting, "that no slaves be imported into any of the thirteen United Colonies." *Then was British policy rebuked, and British power defied.*

The trade was resumed after this, and was not to be finally closed till 1808 – the time limited by the Federal Constitution. During this period, several of the States, Northern and Southern, engaged in the business of importation, which continued up to the time for its final termination. Georgia, in May, 1798 (ten years before the trade could be arrested by Congress), enacted, among her fundamental laws: "There shall be no future importation of slaves into this State from Africa, or any foreign place, after the first day of October next." This, perhaps, is the earliest instance of any one of the thirteen States incorporating in its constitution its determination not to allow the importation to be longer continued within its jurisdiction. And it is probable that since the trade has become contraband, fewer successful efforts have been made to introduce Africans into Georgia than any other slave-holding State. Georgia was the last of the thirteen colonies to adopt African slavery. The colony was settled in 1733. In it slavery was prohibited by law until 1749-50. Thus, it is seen that Georgia was not only the last colony to adopt the institution, but the first, perhaps, to arrest the abuses connected with it.

CHAPTER FOUR
Laws of the States – Operations of the Church

Remarks

The object of this chapter is to present a brief abstract of the laws of the States in which slavery exists, in so far as concerns the life and personal security of the slave, and the results, as well as they could be ascertained, of the efforts of the Church in favor of the Negro, both in the United States and in Africa. This exhibit, although not as full in some of its statements as we could wish, nevertheless challenges the admiration of every philanthropist, and cannot but receive, as it should, the approbation of the humane and enlightened everywhere, and of all countries.

Situated as the Negro was in his native country, and in the hands of the importer, we behold a human being, than whom no one stood more in need of a friend, and at the same time no one was so destitute of a friend. It is said that the darkest hour of the night is the one that immediately precedes the light of day. In the case of the Negro this was no figure of speech. With him it was a solemn reality; for his hard lot felt its greatest pressure while he was on board the transport-ship. The moment his foot made an impression in American soil, his fortune turned – the melioration of his condition commenced. As soon as he passed into the hands of his permanent owner, he found a friend, a father, who instantly commenced the healing of his wounds. From that day to this, his condition has continued steadily to improve; and we remark, that there has been no period in his history when greater and more successful efforts were being made for him than those of the present time.

There never was a human being whose character and circumstances (respecting what they formerly were, and what they now are), presents so strong a contrast as is observable in the case of the American slave. He was brought to us a naked, ignorant heathen – *a savage* – but one short remove from the brute: now "he is clothed and in his right mind." He is a Christian by education, often by profession. Were it not that he has been with us from the beginning, he never could be recognized as the descendant of African ancestors. There is nothing to awaken surprise in all this, however, when it is remembered that the State, the Church, the master and his family, have been laboriously engaged in working out these results.

We do not pretend to say that there are no inconveniences, irregularities, perhaps improprieties connected with the slavery of the South. That such things exist, we readily allow. What institution is without them? Even the Church has its hypocrites, who, in these days of abolitionism, are vastly multiplied. But, we assert, with all the firmness of truth, that these things have been largely exaggerated by the designing; that they have been greatly reduced from their original magnitude; and that the people of the South are now engaged doing everything that can be done for the purpose of correcting these irregularities altogether. Amendments in the practical workings of the institution are being constantly and extensively made; and these efforts would have been much more rapid and effective, had the people of the South been let alone in the management of the institution. But they have been balked and embarrassed by those "busy bodies in other men's matters," the slave's worst enemies, the treacherous, traitorous abolitionists.

Webster defines the term slave thus: "A person who is wholly subject to the will of another; one who has no freedom of action, but whose person and services are wholly under the control of another." This definition has its shades of meaning distinctly reflected in what a very distinguished English author says: "Pure and proper slavery does not, nay, cannot subsist in England; such, I mean, whereby an absolute and unlimited power is given to the master, over the life and fortune of the slave." [Blackstone could not have said so much respecting the British dependencies – to wit, the West Indies.] The kind of slavery here spoken of is the kind of slavery that now subsists in Africa. It is the kind of slavery that subsisted while the slave was in the hands of the importer, who regarded him as an article of merchandise simply; *but it is not the slavery of the United States. Such slavery does not now, never did, and never can, subsist with us.*

It is necessary to pure and proper slavery that the master should have absolute and unlimited power over the life of the slave. This power has never been allowed in the United States. The security of the life of the slave has not been trusted to the interests of the master, nor to his humanity. The law takes the life (and, as will be seen from the following extracts, much besides that relates to the slave's well being) under its own protection. That it trusts to no man; there let it remain.

But we may be asked, What is the condition of the Negro in the Southern States, if it be not slavery in the highest sense of the term? We reply, It is a peculiar condition of servitude, regulated by law, having no parallel in profane history, instituted of God, for the education and training of the African here, for his personal enjoyment of civil and religious liberty, compatible with his condition; and for the other purpose of constituting him an agent, through whom his native country is to be redeemed from its deep degradation. Who objects to this?

The law abhors cruelty and punishes indiscriminately, all who are guilty of it. It will be perceived upon reflection, that the law trusts the master with no more power over his slave, than it trusts to a master over his apprentice, or to a father over his child. If it becomes necessary to use power beyond this, the law reserves to itself the exercise of that power. If punishment, beyond moderate correction (which does not involve the loss of life or limb, or extend to the mutilation of the person), must be inflicted, the law inflicts it.

But, it may be said that there are hard masters, who abuse the power intrusted to them by law; that there sometimes occur excesses amongst slave-holders: we have no concealments on this subject, we allow that there are occurrences of the kind alluded to; but we affirm that these occurrences rarely arise from wantonness. It must be remembered, that we have to control a race of human beings who are under the influence of the most depraved and vicious propensities that ever marked the character of the debased: individuals of which race seem to be incapable of redemption, either by kindness or severity.

In view of the law, the efforts of the Church, and the humanity of masters generally, if not universally, we assert, that the slavery of the South is an anomaly; that is to say, it is without a parallel in the history of human slavery: therefore, to pass a correct judgment on the subject, requires the knowledge of it, in all its parts and particulars: a knowledge which few, if any out of the South, possess; and for the want of which, many of our Northern fellow-citizens have proceeded to condemn the institution.

It is not our intention here to do more than show, that in each State the law recognizes no difference, in its solicitude for human life, between the free white citizen and the Negro slave (that is to say, the law regards the taking the life of the one, as highly criminal as the taking the life of the other). We shall do no more than this, for the reason, that each State has adopted a system of its own; to insert the entire system, or an abridgment of it, of each State, would unnecessarily incumber the subject. The various systems of the States result in the establishment of general principles.

We deem it proper, however, here to remark, that in all cases below those affecting life or limb, the proceedings are had before justices of the peace. These officers issue warrants for the arrest of the accused; subpoena witnesses for and against him; and if, after a fair and impartial investigation, it appears that the accused is guilty, they are authorized to proceed to order the infliction of corporal punishment.

It will be admitted by all who are acquainted with the history of British emancipation, that Wilberforce was the most conspicuous person connected with it, and that his untiring efforts did more than those of anyone else; perhaps more than all the others engaged, in consummating that object. It would be easy to show how the British importers of African slaves, in and out of Parliament, thwarted and embarrassed his movements from 1788 to the year 1808, when, by the Constitution of the United States, the business was rendered profitless; but that is not our object. We introduce here the name of Wilberforce, for the purpose of presenting the following brief but very significant quotation; he says, "Under the protection of the law, is in fact to be a freeman." The system of slavery against which Wilberforce struggled, afforded no legal protection to slaves. Such is not the system of the South.

But ample as the laws are for the protection of the slave (servant is the proper word), he finds great security in public opinion: this is always active; always on the side of the people; always does the slave justice, and always forbids cruelty. Let the reader collect in his mind the vast security thrown around the slave by the State, the Church, the master's interest and public opinion, and then condemn the slavery of the South, if he will; we are content.

In each of the slave-holding States, the laws for the trial of the question of freedom are so ample and easy, that it is impossible to hold a free Negro in slavery, in either of them. This is an occurrence but seldom heard of, because the laws, in this respect, are but seldom violated.

Section 1

Delaware

"Any two justices of the peace for the county, shall have jurisdiction to try and punish any slave, for the offence of stealing, taking and carrying away, any goods, chattels, effects, bank-note,

money, bill, promissory note, check, order, bond or written con-
tract for the payment of money, or delivery of goods, or of receiving, or concealing, any such stolen property, knowing it to be
stolen, or taken by robbery."

[In all higher crimes than those punishable by justices of
the peace, an accused slave is tried in the same manner as a free
white person: the bill of indictment against the accused must contain the allegation of his being a slave, &c. On the trial, the master
has the right to defend the slave, by employing counsel, selecting
the jury, &c.]

Maryland

"That whensoever any Negro, Indian or mulatto slave,
shall hereafter be charged with any pilfering or stealing, or any
other crime or misdemeanor whereof the county court might have
cognizance, it shall and may be lawful for any one of the justices,
of the provincial or county courts, upon complaint made before
him, to cause such Negro, Indian or mulatto slave, so offending,
to be brought immediately before him, or any other justice of the
peace for the county where such offence is committed, who upon
due proof made against any such Negro or mulatto slave, of any
of the crimes as aforesaid, such justice is hereby authorized and
empowered to award and cause to be inflicted, according to the
nature of the crime, such punishment, by whipping, as he shall
think fit, not exceeding forty lashes."

"That every slave committing any of the felonies here-
inbefore mentioned [crimes involving the loss of life or limb], or
any other offence which may by law subject such slave to the pains
of death, shall be committed to the sheriff of the county where the
offence shall be committed, and that at the next assizes, or county
court, which shall first happen to be held for the county where the
offence shall be committed, the justices of assize, or either of
them, or county court which shall first happen, shall and may by
virtue of this act, try every such offender or offenders according
to law, and upon the conviction of the offender or offenders, upon

his, her, or their voluntary confession, or the verdict of a jury, upon the testimony of one or more legal or credible witness or witnesses, or even the testimony, or the evidence of other slaves, corroborated with such pregnant circumstances as shall convince and satisfy the jury who shall try the fact of the guilt of such slave or slaves, to give judgment according to the nature and quality of the offence."

[The laws of Maryland, on this subject, are enforced in the District of Columbia.]

Missouri

"Every person who shall cruelly or inhumanly torture, beat, wound or abuse any slave in his employment, or under his charge, power or control, whether belonging to himself or another, shall on conviction be punished by imprisonment in a county jail, not exceeding one year, or by fine, not exceeding one thousand dollars, or by both, such fine and imprisonment.

"If any slave, or his master, in any case cognizable before a justice of the peace, shall require a jury, the justice shall cause such jury to be summoned, sworn and empannelled, who shall determine the facts and assess the punishment, in case of conviction; and the justice shall enter judgment and cause the same to be executed."

Virginia

"The justices of every county or corporation shall be justices of oyer and terminer, for trying slaves charged with felony; which trials shall be by five at least, without juries, upon legal evidence, at such times as the sheriffs or other officers shall appoint, not being less than five, nor more than ten days, after the offenders shall have been committed to jail. No slave shall be condemned in any such case, unless all of the justices, sitting upon his or her trial, shall agree in opinion that the prisoner is guilty, after assigning him or her counsel, in his or her defence, whose fee, amounting to not less than five, nor more than twenty-five dollars, at the discretion of the justices sitting upon said trial, shall be paid by the owner of the slave. Provided always, That when judgment of death shall be passed upon any such offender, there shall be thirty days at least, between the time of passing judgment and the day of execution, except in cases of conspiracy, insurrection or rebellion."

[Other offences (not involving life or limb), punishable by justices of the peace, by whipping, not exceeding forty stripes.]

"And in cases when any slave or slaves shall be tried and convicted for any crime which may affect life, the court before whom such trials shall be had, shall cause the testimony for and against every such slave to be entered of record, and a copy of the whole proceedings to be transmitted forthwith to the executive."

Kentucky

"If the owner of any slave shall treat him cruelly and inhumanly, so as, in the opinion of a jury, to endanger the life or limb of such slave, or materially to affect his health; or shall not supply his slave with sufficient wholesome food and raiment, such slave shall be taken and sold for the benefit of the owner."

"The final trial of a slave, for offences punished with death, shall be had in the circuit court of the county in which the offence was committed; and he shall be tried by a jury, in the same mode and manner as free persons are tried.

"The master or owner of any slave may, on the trial of his slave for crimes or misdemeanors, defend him,

"When any slave shall be charged with felony, the master or owner may bail such slave, in those cases in which free persons are bailable, according to the laws regulating bail in criminal cases.

"It shall be the duty of the master or owner, personal representative, or guardian of such owner, to employ counsel to defend a slave when tried in the circuit court. If no counsel be employed, the court shall assign counsel to defend him."

[Crimes below those denominated felonies, are punished

by whipping, and may be inflicted by order of a justice of the peace, or other court before whom the offender may be tried.]

North Carolina

"The offence of killing a slave shall be homicide, and shall partake of the same degree of guilt, when accompanied with the like circumstances, that homicide does at common law."

"Every slave or free person of color who shall hereafter be convicted of any felony, for which no specific punishment is pre-scribed by statute, and which is now allowed the benefit of clergy, shall be imprisoned, at the discretion of the court, not exceeding two years; and in addition to such imprisonment, the court may sentence the convict to receive one or more public whippings, or to stand in the pillory, or if a free Negro, to pay a fine, regard being had to the circumstances of each case.

"When a slave shall be apprehended or indicted for any offence, whereof the superior court has original jurisdiction, his owner, if known, shall have ten days' notice of the trial, in order that he may have an opportunity of defending his slave; the cost of which notice, and all other costs attending the trial for the slave, shall be paid by the owner, if such slave, being a free man, would be liable to the payment thereof. And if the owner refuse to pay the same, execution in the name of the State may issue against such owner.

"When the owner of any slave who may be tried, in virtue of this chapter, shall not be known, or cannot be ascertained, or shall reside out of the State, the Court shall appoint counsel to appear for the prisoner, who shall be allowed the same fees as the attorney for the State is allowed for such criminal prosecutions; after which, the trial may proceed in the same manner as if the owner had been notified agreeably to the directions of this chap-ter; and the fees for the counsel, clerk and sheriff, shall be paid by the county having cognizance of the offence, as any other county charges."

"Whenever any slave shall be convicted before a justice of

the peace of any offence, the master on behalf of the slave may appeal to the next county or superior court, on entering into sufficient recognizance for the slave, and giving good security, as in other cases of appeals.

"The superior court shall have exclusive original jurisdiction of all felonies and other offences committed by slaves, which, by section thirty-two, arc not assigned for trial before a justice of the peace; and the trial shall be conducted in like manner as the trials of free men for the same offence; and moreover, the jurors shall be slave-owners."

South Carolina

"That upon complaint made to any justice of the peace, of any heinous or grievous crime, committed by any slave or slaves, as murder, burglary, robbery, burning of houses, or any other lesser crimes, as killing, or stealing any neat or other cattle, maiming one the other, stealing of fowls, provisions, or such like trespasses, or injuries, the said justice shall issue out his warrant for apprehending the offender or offenders, and for all persons to come before him that can give evidence; and if upon examination, it probably appeareth that the apprehended person is guilty, he shall commit him or them to prison, or immediately proceed to trial of the said slave or slaves, according to the form hereafter specified, or take security for his or their forthcoming, as the case shall require, and also, to certify to the justice next to him, the said course, and to require him, by virtue of this act, to associate himself to him, which the said justice is hereby required to do, and they so associated are to issue their summons to three sufficient freeholders, acquainting them with the matter, and appointing them a day, hour and place, when and where the same shall be heard and determined, at which day, hour and place, the said justice and freeholders shall cause the offender and evidences to come before them, and if they on hearing the matter (the said freeholders being by the said justices, first sworn to judge uprightly and according to evidence), and diligently weighing and examining all evidences, proofs and testimonies, and in case of murder only if on violent presumption and circumstances, they shall find such Negro or other slave or slaves, guilty thereof, they shall give sentence of death, if the crime, by law, deserves the same, and forthwith by their warrant cause immediate execution to be done, by the common or any other executioner, in such manner as they shall think fit, the kind of death to be inflicted to be left to their judgment and discretion; and if the crime committed shall not deserve death, they shall then condemn and adjudge the criminal or criminals to any other punishment, but not extending to limb or disabling him, without a particular law directing such punishment, and shall forthwith order execution to be done accordingly."

Tennessee

"The master, owner, or overseer of any slave to be arraigned and tried, may appear at the trial, and make what just defence he can for such slave or slaves, so that such defence does not relate to any formality in the proceedings on the trial."

"Where any slave or slaves shall hereafter commit any offence which is not by law declared capital, the justice before whom he or she is taken shall, and he is hereby authorized and empowered, forthwith to issue subpoenas, if necessary, to compel the attendance of witnesses, and proceed immediately upon the trial of such slave or slaves, in a summary way, and to pass sentence, and award execution. *Provided*, The punishment shall extend no farther than ordering the offender to be publicly whipped, not exceeding forty lashes; and when the offence for which any slave shall be apprehended is declared by law to be capital, such offending slave shall be committed to jail, and stand his or her trial by a court, in the way prescribed by law."

"The circuit court, in addition to the jurisdiction conferred by the Act to which this is a supplement, shall hereafter have exclusive original jurisdiction of all offences committed by slaves, which are by law punishable with death; and so much of the Acts of Assembly as requires a special court, consisting of justices, to try such cases in the first instance, be repealed. In all such cases, the trials of slaves shall be in all respects conducted and disposed of in the same manner, and under the same laws and rules that now govern such cases after they are taken into the circuit courts by appeal. *Provided,* That such slave or slaves shall not be tried before a jury until an indictment or presentment is first found by the grand jury. *And provided,* That if the master of the slave so tried does not employ counsel in his defence, the court shall assign him counsel, and shall fix the amount of his fee; and such fee shall be recoverable by such counsel against the owner or owners of such slave, by action of debt. *And provided,* That the owner of said slave shall not be liable to pay the costs of said prosecution."

Georgia

"Any person who shall maliciously dismember, or deprive a slave of life, shall suffer such punishment as would be inflicted in case the like offence had been committed on a free white person; and on the like proof, except in case of insurrection by such slave, and unless such death should happen by accident, in giving such slave moderate correction.

"In all cases, the killing or maiming of a slave, or person of color, or Indian, in amity with the United States, shall be put upon the same footing of criminality as the killing or maiming of a white person.

"If any person or persons whomsoever shall maliciously deprive a slave or slaves of life, he, she, or they so offending shall be prosecuted by indictment in the superior court of the county in which such offence may have been committed, in like manner as if the person or persons charged had perpetrated a like offence on any free white person or persons whomsoever; and on all such trials the same rules of law and evidence shall obtain, as on other trials for murder. And if, upon trial for such offence, any person or persons shall be found guilty of murder, he, she, or they shall suffer such punishment as would be inflicted in case the like offence had been committed on a free white person; that is to say, shall be hanged, without the benefit of clergy. And if found guilty of manslaughter, shall be punished by branding [changed to penitentiary imprisonment], in like manner as is usual in cases where any person or persons is or are convicted of manslaughter, committed on a free white person or persons, except in case of insurrection by such slave, and unless such death should happen by accident, in giving such slave moderate correction."

[The trial of a slave, in cases in which his life is involved, is had in the same court, and conducted in the same manner, as that of a white person. The master is allowed to appear on the part of his slave, employ counsel, select the jury, arrange the evidence, &c.]

"Any owner or employer of a slave or slaves, who shall cruelly treat such slave or slaves, by unnecessary and excessive whipping, by withholding proper food and sustenance, by requiring greater labor from such slave or slaves than he, she, or they are able to perform; or by not affording proper clothing, whereby the health of such slave or slaves may be injured and impaired; or cause, or permit the same to be done; every such owner or employer shall be guilty of a misdemeanor, and, on conviction, shall be punished by fine, or imprisonment in the common jail of the county, or both, at the discretion of the court."

Florida

"In the trial of any slave in the circuit court, the same rules and regulations shall be observed as are observed in the trial of free persons."

"It shall be the duty of the courts of this State, charged with the trial of slaves, to assign and appoint counsel to defend any slave tried before them, in all cases where the master of any slave, his agent or guardian, fails or refuses to employ an attorney to defend such slave; and all such attorneys shall receive for their services, from the master, owner, or guardian of such slave, any sum that the court shall deem reasonable – not exceeding fifty dollars – which shall be recoverable as other debts of like magnitude."

[In all cases below those denominated capital, justices of the peace preside. Punishment inflicted by them extends to whipping.]

Alabama.

The State constitution provides, that, "They [the General Assembly] shall have full power to oblige the owners of slaves to treat them with humanity; to provide for them necessary food and clothing; to abstain from all injuries to them, extending to life or limb; and in case of their neglect or refusal, to have such slave or slaves sold for the benefit of the owner or owners."

The constitution also provides, that, "In the prosecution of slaves for crimes of a higher grade than petit larceny, the General Assembly shall have no power to deprive them of an impartial trial by a petit jury."

A farther constitutional provision is, "Any person who shall maliciously dismember, or deprive a slave of life, shall suffer such punishment as would be inflicted in case the like offence had been committed on a free white person, and on the like proof; except in case of insurrection of such slave."

A provisional statute is, "That whenever any slave shall be brought before a justice of the county court, or of the peace, for the commission of any offence against the penal laws of this State, of a higher grade than petit larceny; if the justice after examination, should think there are just and probable grounds of suspicion of the guilt or criminality of the offender, he shall immediately commit such slave to jail; and he is hereby empowered and directed to issue a summons to the sheriff of the county, to summons the justices of the county court, and a jury of twelve good and lawful men of the vicinage, to meet at the court-house of said county; neither of whom shall be master of said slave, or related to the master, or prosecutor of such slave, in any degree, which should be a cause of challenge to a juryman, in a trial of a free person. And such court and jury shall proceed in the trial of such slave, without presentment or indictment. And no slave shall be condemned, unless he be found guilty by a jury, after allowing him or her counsel, in his or her defence, whose fee, amounting to ten dollars, shall be paid by the owner of the slave: provided always that when judgment of death shall be passed upon such offender, there shall be thirty days, at least, between the time of passing judgment and the day of execution; except in cases of conspiracy, insurrection, or rebellion."

Another statutory provision is, "That no cruel or unusual punishment shall be inflicted on any slave within this territory. And any owner of slaves authorizing or permitting the same, shall on conviction thereof, before any court having cognizance, be fined according to the nature of the offence, and at the discretion of the court, in a sum not exceeding two hundred dollars, to and for the use of this territory.

"That the trial of a slave for felony, or any capital offence, shall be in all respects similar to the trial of a free citizen or inhabitant, for the like offence; except that the jury, or two-thirds at least thereof, empannelled for such trial, shall be composed of owners of slaves."

Mississippi

"No cruel or unusual punishment shall be inflicted on any slave within this State. And any master, or other person, entitled to the service of any slave, who shall inflict such cruel or unusual punishment, or shall authorize or permit the same to be inflicted, shall on conviction thereof, before any court having cognizance, be fined according to the magnitude of the offence, at the discretion of the court, in any sum not exceeding five hundred dollars, to be paid into the treasury of the State, for the use and benefit of the literary fund.

"The justices of every county or corporation court in this State, shall be justices of oyer and terminer, for the trial of slaves charged with felony; which trials shall be at the court-house of the proper county, and at such time as the sheriff or other officer, whose duty it shall be to summon such court, shall appoint; unless the same be at a stated term of the county or corporation court, not being less than five, nor more than ten days after the offender or offenders shall have been committed to jail. And when any slave or slaves shall be committed for any offence, which by this act is declared to be capital, and punishable with death, it shall be the duty of such sheriff or other officer, to summon twenty-four good and lawful men of the vicinage, twelve of whom at least shall be slave-holders, in their own right: and neither the master of such slave or slaves, or any person related to him, or to the prosecutor, shall be one of the persons so summoned, to be and appear at the time and place when and where the said court shall be convened, for the trial of such offender or offenders; from which number a jury of twelve shall be selected, sworn and empannelled; and such court and jury shall proceed to the trial of the slave or slaves charged as aforesaid, upon legal evidence, without presentment or indictment, and on conviction by the verdict of a jury, the court shall proceed to pass sentence, and order execution thereof, according to law.

"In the trial of slaves, the right of challenge of jurors for cause, shall be allowed to both parties, according to the rules of law prescribed in other cases of trial by jury, and a peremptory challenge on the part of the prisoner, to the number of six, in capital cases.

"In the trial of any slave or slaves, for a capital crime, the court shall have power to grant new trials, according to the rules established in other criminal cases." [Counsel for the accused must be appointed by the court.]

"When judgment of death shall be passed upon any slave or slaves, there shall be twenty days at least between the time of passing judgment, and the day of execution, except in cases of conspiracy, insurrection or rebellion."

Louisiana

"When slaves are prosecuted in the name of the State, for

offences they have committed, notice must be given to their masters."

[In this State when a master is convicted of cruel treatment of his slaves, the judge may pronounce, in addition to the penalty established by law, in such cases, that the slave shall be sold to some more humane owner, "in order to place him out of the reach of the power which his master has abused."]

"The slave is entirely subject to the will of his master, who may correct and chastise him, though not with unusual rigor, nor so as to maim or mutilate him, or to expose him to the danger of loss of life, or to cause his death."

Arkansas

The State constitution provides that the Legislature shall have power "to oblige the owner of any slave or slaves, to treat them with humanity: and in the prosecution of slaves for any crime, they shall not be deprived of an impartial jury; and any slave who shall be convicted of a capital offence, shall suffer the same degree of punishment as would be inflicted on a free white person, and no other; and courts of justice before whom slaves shall be tried, shall assign them counsel for their defence."

"In all cases of felony, the slave committing the same shall be tried in the same court, and the same rules of evidence observed, as in cases of white persons committing the like offence; excepting that slaves may be witnesses for and against slaves."

Texas

The State constitution provides that the Legislature "shall have full power to pass laws, which will oblige the owners of slaves to treat them with humanity; to provide for their necessary food and clothing; to abstain from all injuries to them, extending to life or limb; and in case of their neglect or refusal to comply with the directions of such laws, to have such slave or slaves taken from such owner, and sold for the benefit of such owner or owners."

Another constitutional provision is – "In the prosecution of slaves for crimes of a higher grade than petit larceny, the legislature shall have no power to deprive them of an impartial trial by a petit jury."

And further – "Any person who shall maliciously dismember, or deprive a slave of life, shall suffer such punishment as would be inflicted in case the like offence had been committed upon a free white person, and on the like proof – except in case of insurrection of such slaves."

"That [all crimes, below those denominated capital] known to the common law of England, committed by slaves, shall be triable before the county courts, and on conviction shall be punished at the discretion of said courts, so as not to extend to life or limb." [Cases of the kind here mentioned are tried by juries.]

[Crimes of a higher degree than those triable in the county courts, are tried in the district courts; these trials are by juries. In such cases, if the owner refuses or neglects to employ counsel, counsel is assigned the accused by the court. The proceedings are the same as in cases of white persons.]

"That if any person or persons shall murder any slave, or so cruelly treat the same as to cause death, the same shall be felony, and punished as in other cases of murder.

"That if any person or persons shall cruelly or unreasonably treat or abuse any slave belonging to him, her, or them, or to another or others, he, she, or they, and each of them, shall be liable to indictment or presentment, as for a misdemeanor, in the district court, and on conviction thereof, may be fined for each and every such offence, not less than twenty dollars, nor more than five hundred dollars."

There is no branch of the law, particularly in the older States, that requires revision more than those on the subject of slaves. Many obsolete laws are permitted to remain upon the statute-books, which greatly embarrass the subject, so that it becomes, in some instances, almost, perhaps to some, entirely incomprehensible.

Section 2

Operations of the Church

The following statements will show the results of the efforts of the different churches relative to the Negro, both in the United States and in Africa.

Methodist Episcopal Church (South)

173 Missions. – The Missionary report of 1855 says, "Increased confidence is everywhere manifested towards these missions, and constantly increasing facilities afforded our missionaries by those who are most directly interested, as the owners of the slaves. Every year the field is enlarging. From every direction the cry is heard, 'Come over and help us.' More plantations are opened than can be occupied. The planters, in many instances, contribute liberally to their support."

145 Missionaries. – This Church employs some 270 missionaries; that is to say, 125 more than those employed among the colored people. For the support of all her missionaries, this Church disbursed in 1855, $172,654.53.

53 Church edifices. – These buildings are generally erected by a number of planters uniting for that purpose.

17,883 Children under instruction.

170,150 Church members.

Methodist Episcopal Church (North)

This Church, several years ago, declined any farther effort in favor of the people of color in the Southern States (not formally to be sure, but effectually); and now, so far as respects these people, this Church presents the astonishing fact of a Methodist Church depriving itself of access to a small field of labor at home, containing some three millions of souls! For these souls this Church makes, at present, no effort whatever; nor is it at all probable, perhaps not possible, that it ever will hereafter. Behold the effects of abolitionism!

At the time of the separation of the Churches, North and South, the operations in Africa were left with the Church North.

The following statement will show the condition of things in Africa:

Liberia Mission. – 1855

22 Missionaries. – This mission "extends back from the coast up the principal rivers, and has access, not only to the inhabitants which have emigrated from America, but also to some one hundred and forty or one hundred and fifty thousand natives."

1,449 Church members.

21 Local preachers.

22 Teachers, male and female.

3 Seminaries of learning, to wit, Monrovia Seminary, Cape Palmas Seminary, and Millsburgh Female Academy.

1 Labor school at White Plains, on the St. Paul's river.

The report for 1855 says, "We have a number of day-schools in the mission, and Sunday-schools in every pastoral charge. And besides these, arrangements are made to receive native youth into the families of nearly all our missionaries, that they may receive the rudiments of instruction, and the first elements of Christian civilization." The amount disbursed in 1855, was $36,407.

Baptist Church

Our efforts to procure reliable information with regard to this Church, both among the slaves of the South and the people of Africa, have resulted in the following statements:

One of the corresponding secretaries of the Board of Foreign Missions, writes, "In the slave-holding States we have about 500,000 church-members, and perhaps one-half, or approaching that proportion, may be put down as colored.

"In all the various departments of service, about thirty men, all colored men, excepting five. Our schools, weekday and Sunday, in Africa, number about five hundred scholars. We expend in the foreign missions about $36,000, nearly two-thirds, or more than one-half, in Africa. The Domestic Board will expend about the same amount in the home field. Our local associations probably expend about $75,000 more, in the home field."

The corresponding secretary of the Board of Domestic Missions writes, "In reply I have to state, that I am unable to give you any satisfactory information on the subject of your inquiry. The Board of which I am secretary, has seven missionaries employed for the benefit of the colored people: two of these are in Georgia; two in Alabama; one in Baltimore, and one in Washington City; the two latter are colored men."

Presbyterian Church

Our information relating to the operations of this Church is as follows:

The statistics in regard to Liberia, asked for in yours of the 25th inst., are the following: three missionaries (ministers of the Gospel), two of them white and one colored, in connection with the Presbytery of Tuscaloosa.

3 Licentiate preachers, colored.

5 Colored teachers.

1 High school, with fifteen scholars.

4 English schools, one hundred and fifty-three scholars.

4 Sabbath schools, one hundred scholars.

4 Churches, with one hundred and thirty-nine communicants.

These missionaries and schools are supported by the Board of Foreign Missions of the Presbyterian Church. A number of special donations for the African Mission, is received from the colored church-members of the South.

In the Presbyterian Church in the United States there are 10,419 colored communicants.

The secretary of the Domestic Board writes:

1. That the Presbyterian Church has in the slave-holding States 9,533 colored communicants.

2. That the Church has in said States 801 ministers of the Gospel; 150 of whom were domestic missionaries, who give more or less attention to the colored population.

3. That there was reported for domestic missionary purposes, by the churches in said States, the sum of $32,863; of which amount $19,028 was contributed to the Board of Domestic Missions.

We have to regret the meager and unsatisfactory condition of our Church information. Our desire was to present in detail the operations of the Methodist (North and South), the Baptist, the Presbyterian and the Episcopal Churches amongst the slaves in the United States and the people of Africa. We wished to show the number of church members; the numbers forming the congregations; the number of schools (week-day and Sunday); the mode of teaching; the number of preachers and teachers employed; the number of scholars; the amount of money raised, disbursed, &c,, by each Church; but the manner in which these things have been kept by the Churches has almost totally defeated our object. The Churches appear to be content to perform the work without troubling themselves much about details. There has been no manifested unwillingness on the part of those to whom we have applied to supply us with the information desired, except by the Episcopal Church; those of this Church to whom we applied declined to respond to our inquiries.

So strong is our desire to present the whole of this information, that we yet indulge the hope that members of these respective Churches will compile tables containing it, which we may present in a subsequent edition. The cause of truth and justice requires that such information should be published.

Section 3

From the foregoing exhibit it will be seen that the State

and the Church have done, and are doing much for the protection and the improvement of the slave; yet there is much necessary to his well-being that must be done by the master and his family.

It will be admitted that one of the strongest motives that induces human conduct is personal interest; this strong motive works in favor of the slave. Being, as he is, the property of his master, it is the master's interest to provide for his comfort, and to preserve his health; hence the necessity of providing him with a sufficient quantity of wholesome food, and clothing suitable to the season (It is a well-known fact, that there is less sickness and mortality amongst the colored than amongst the white population, according to numbers). When a slave falls sick, it is the master's interest, leaving out motives of humanity, that he should be restored to health as speedily as possible; hence, as soon as he becomes too unwell to labor, the family physician is immediately called in, and nurses are employed to attend upon him; all this is done under the supervision of the master and his family. Many large bills are paid to physicians for their attention to slaves alone.

The slaves always find strong friends in the white children of the family, by whom many of them are taught to read. It is a scene of some interest to behold the teaching process. A large class of grown and ungrown persons is arranged in proper order before its teacher; words are given out to each individual, which they are required to spell. Some inattentive scholar is soon detected by his inability to perform his task. He is tried over and over again, without success, until the little teacher becomes worried and impatient, and more attention is promised on the part of the scholar. The proceeding is then continued with the others of the class. We allude to this, or something like it, as a general arrangement.

As soon as a slave learns to read, he procures a New Testament (this is their favorite book; with its parables, allegories and metaphors they are delighted), over which he will pore for hours together. It is a fact worthy of mention, that not an infidel or sceptic is to be found amongst slaves; sinners may be found amongst them in large numbers, but they invariably entertain correct views of the principles of Christianity, and acknowledge their truth. They leave infidelity and scepticism to those of superior intellectual endowments.

CHAPTER FIVE
Colonization – Sierra Leone – Liberia

Section 1

"Ethiopia shall soon stretch out her hands unto God." – This prophecy is now in the course of rapid and successful fulfilment.

The idea of Christianizing Africa by means of native preachers, educated in, and sent from the United States, was conceived by the Rev. Samuel Hopkins, D.D. This divine was the founder of the sect called Hopkinsians, whose creed may be summed up in the following brief and beautiful sentence: "All true virtue or real holiness, consists in disinterested benevolence." Dr. Hopkins died at Newport, in the State of Rhode Island, where he had resided many years, in 1803.

Before the Revolutionary war, the people of Newport were largely engaged in the African slave-trade; indeed, this was the principal source of their commerce and wealth. Dr. Hopkins himself had been a slave-holder, but had sold his slave property before he came to Newport to reside.

After long and patient investigation, Dr. Hopkins became thoroughly convinced that the slave-trade was iniquitous; this he announced to his congregation in a prepared discourse. Alexander says, "Although the people of Newport were deeply engaged in the slave-trade, and derived their wealth very much from this source, and his own people [those of his church] as much as others, yet he determined to lift up his voice against it, and, accordingly, several years before the commencement of the Revolutionary war, he preached a sermon to his people, pointedly condemning this iniquitous traffic."

Dr. Hopkins did not stop at the mere announcement of his convictions, he desired to reduce them to practical operation. Accordingly he applied the funds arising from the sale of his slave property, "to the scheme of educating Africans, to be sent back to their own country to instruct their countrymen. And as he knew that a solitary individual could accomplish but little in such a work, he set himself to form an African Missionary Society, to educate and send out missionaries to carry the Gospel to that benighted region."

Dr. Hopkins soon engaged in this enterprise Dr. Ezra Stiles, then pastor of a congregation in Newport, afterwards president of Yale College. These ministers issued a circular letter, setting forth their benevolent intentions, which soon brought them funds sufficient to enable them to educate Bristol Yamma and John Quamine, two Africans, members of the First Congregational Church in Newport. Yamma and Quamine were sent to Princeton, New Jersey, "to be for a season under the tuition of the Rev. Dr. Witherspoon, the president of the New Jersey College." Alexander says, "Besides the two already mentioned (who now only waited for a good opportunity of sailing for Africa), there was a third, named Salmur Nuba, a member of the Second Congregational Church in Newport, then under the pastoral charge of Dr. Stiles." The Revolutionary war coming on, however, defeated these benevolent undertakings – the missionaries did not go out at that time.

Here is sufficient proof to show, that the Christianizing Africa, by means of native preachers, educated in the United States, is an American idea; at least, the idea first became a reality here. And from this idea, it is altogether probable, flowed the great conception of colonizing Africa with the free persons of color in England and the United States; indeed, colonization seems to be but the maturity of the idea.

Section 2

Sierra Leone. – We have not the proof necessary to enable us to assert unqualifiedly, that the idea of Dr. Hopkins led to colonization; but we have said that the truth was probably so; we have said so, because Dr. Hopkins and Granville Sharp (who should be regarded as the father of African colonization in England), were in close and familiar correspondence, during the life of Dr. Hopkins; it is probable, therefore, that the subject of colonization was discussed between them: however this may be, Dr. Hopkins and Mr. Sharp were engaged in one work – a great enterprise, affording sufficient honor for both and for all.

During the war of the Revolution, many slaves were induced to leave their owners and take refuge in the British army; they followed the army out of the country. The injustice of this act was acknowledged, and as far as it could be, atoned for, by England paying for the property carried away. (It is singular that the same thing occurred in the war of 1812!) The Negroes were made to believe that they would not only be free, but amply provided for, with all the necessaries of easy living, when they arrived in England. These promises were sufficient to induce them to leave their masters (but few Negroes like to work), but they were promises never realized by them. When they arrived in London, like those that now escape from their masters into the Northern States, and Canada, they came to the knowledge that they would have to work much harder than formerly, to secure the same amount of good. Disappointed, they roamed about the streets, begging from door to door, and pilfering what they could. Poverty, in this case, as in all other cases, brought with it its attendant concomitants, and the condition of the Negroes became deplorable. This excited the commiseration of Sharp, Wilberforce, Thornton, Hardcastle, Clarkson and others, whose efforts resulted in the colonization of the Negroes in Africa.

Companies having been organized and chartered in 1787, a district of country was purchased from the native chiefs, as a settlement for the Negroes – it was called Sierra Leone. Sierra Leone is the name of a river, discovered in 1462; it was formerly called Mitomba. "The name Sierra Leone," says Lynch, "was given to the mountain range south of the river, from the fancy that the loud reverberation of thunder in the vallies, resembled the roaring of lions." Sharp called this territory "The Province of Freedom."

The British government, at once, identified itself with this enterprise; it assumed the expense of transporting the Negroes to the colony, and the supplying of them, for six months after their arrival, with such necessaries as their condition required. The first colonists that went out suffered from being too much crowded in their ships; out of four hundred and sixty who embarked, eighty-four died on the passage; and after they had landed, before the close of the rainy season, a hundred more died from the climate. In 1790, the colonists lost their settlement by difficulties with the natives; in 1791 they recovered it.

Some of the Negroes who took refuge in the British army, were conveyed to Nova Scotia. "These," says Alexander, "finding the severe climate of this Northern province uncongenial to their constitutions, and having heard of the colony at Sierra Leone, dispatched a delegate to England, to request that they might also be transported to Africa." These persons were, by the government, conveyed to the colony; they numbered eleven hundred and thirty-one: on the passage from Halifax to England sixty-five died. The Negroes originally from the United States, and the Maroons from the West Indies, made up the colonists of Sierra Leone.

Section 3

In 1794, England and France were at war. "On the 27th of September," says Alexander, "a French squadron made its appearance on the coast, and began to fire on the town. All resistance being vain against such a force, the colony was immediately surrendered into their hands. The conduct of the French commodore and his men was ferocious and even cruel, to this hapless infant colony. They not only seized the goods of the company and of the English residents, but robbed the houses of the poor blacks of whatever they could carry away; and then set the town on fire. Even the church was pillaged, and the medicine-store destroyed; which last proved the severest loss of all. After the first conflagration, a second was ordered, in which the church and all the remaining houses were consumed. And most unfortunately, while the French had possession of the colony, the company's largest ship, the Harpy, came in sight, having on board several passengers, and goods to the amount of £10,000. Observing the demolition of the company's houses, she put back to sea, but was discovered and pursued by the French; and when captured, all the goods were seized, and even the property of the English passengers was also taken. None of these articles were landed, but immediately carried away. What rendered this calamity doubly severe was the fact, that in this vessel the company had sent out a plant-hatch, containing many valuable articles received from the king's collection at Kew, which it was supposed would be likely to grow and flourish in this climate. Two other vessels of the company, employed in the coasting trade, were also taken. All the native chiefs appeared to be afflicted on account of the over-whelming calamity which had befallen the colony, except the slave-dealers: these, from the beginning, viewed the rising colony with an invidious eye, and as they cherished hostile feelings towards it, so they rejoiced in its destruction." Here we see the wreck of the first attempt made for the purpose of redeeming Africa. The pecuniary loss of the colony amounted to about £60,000; and when it is remembered that this occurred just at the commencement of the sickly season, we need not say that the sufferings of the colonists were excessively great. *To the French belongs the honor of this brilliant achievement – the crushing of this defenceless work of benevolence.* The amount of injury done in the colony, and at other places, during this hostile visit, was rated at £400,000. From

the losses sustained the colony slowly recovered, and it is altogether probable that these disasters crippled the energies of the
colony permanently.

"In 1803, it was suggested to the company by the ministry,
that it would be for the benefit of the colony to transfer the civil
and military power from the company to the government. The
cession was accordingly made, and the colony is now under the
authority of a governor who resides at Sierra Leone, appointed by,
and amenable to, the British government."

At the time that the company transferred the colony to the
government, the directors made a report, from which we take the
following extract: "The company have communicated the benefits
flowing from a knowledge of letters, and from Christian instruction, to hundreds of Negroes on the coast of Africa; and by a care-
ful education in this country, they have elevated the character of
several of the children of African chiefs, and directed their minds
to objects of the very first importance to their countrymen. They
have ascertained that the cultivation of every valuable article of
tropical export may be carried on in Africa; that Africans in a state
of freedom are susceptible of the same motives of industry and
laborious exertion, which influence the natives of Europe; and that
some African chiefs are sufficiently enlightened to comprehend,
and sufficiently patriotic to encourage, schemes of improvement.
They have demonstrated that Negroes may be governed by the
same mild laws which are found consistent with the maintenance
of rational liberty, even in this kingdom; and that they may be
safely and advantageously entrusted with the administration of
those laws, not only as jurors, but even as judicial assessors. They
have in some measure retrieved the credit of the British – it may
be added, of the Christian name on the continent of Africa; and
have convinced its inhabitants that there are Englishmen who are
actuated by very different motives from those of self-interest, and
who desire nothing so much as their improvement and happiness.
To conclude, they have established in a central part of Africa a
colony, which appears to be now provided with adequate means
both of defence and subsistence; which, by the blessing of Provi-

dence, may become an emporium of commerce, a school of industry, and a source of knowledge, civilization and religious improvement, to the inhabitants of that continent; and which may hereafter repay to Great Britain the benefits she shall have communicated, by opening a continually increasing market for those manufactures which are now no longer secure of their accustomed vent on the continent of Europe." The colony has continued to become more and more useful, in the great objects of its foundation; and now exercises a large influence for good over many of the surrounding tribes and nations.

There are some important considerations arising from the statements connected with the colonization of Sierra Leone, that require attention before we close this section. There is something astonishing in the fact, that according to English sentiment, what is very properly done by England respecting African colonization, becomes criminal when it is done by the United States (There are some honorable exceptions to this remark). Englishmen cannot see why the free people of color in the United States cannot be allowed quietly to remain where they are, and enjoy the privileges of citizenship, They see no propriety in our urging these persons to seek a home in Liberia. They condemn all this as unkind, if not inhuman. To Englishmen holding these opinions we would say, Why did not England permit the few persons of color in London, her first colonists, to remain where they were? Why were they required to make the first experiment in colonization? If it be commendable in Anglo-Saxons to colonize in Africa their free people of color, how is the doing the same thing by Anglo-Americans blameworthy? We but follow their example! But in this we see, as we are wont to see in all British policy – England must be allowed to do what she pleases, and condemn whom she will, in every instance, and under all circumstances. We rejoice to know, that at last the United States have become worried with this course of injustice, and are determined no longer to submit to it.

And there is another important fact that must be noticed in this connection. How came the Negroes, with whom we are colonizing Liberia, in the United States? *Englishmen brought them here and sold them to us!* We came by them honestly, and are as honestly engaged in seeking their present and future welfare, in our own way. How came England by her colonists? The proprieties of history forbid that we should give the answer to this question in plain language: we submit the answer to English abolitionists, whether they be found in the walks of private life, or exercising governmental functions.

There is one other consideration which must be alluded to here. The primary objects that the people of the United States have in colonizing Liberia, are the good of the colonists individually, and the redemption of Africa. More elevated objects never entered into any enterprise. What, according to all accounts, particularly the extract which we have made from the report of the directors, was the primary object of the colonization of Sierra Leone? The answer is, commercial advantage. Commerce, which is but an incidental consideration with the colonizationists of the United States, forms the paramount object with the colonizationists of England – here lies the difference between the parties. We except a portion of the English Church from the force of the foregoing remark.

Section 4

Liberia. – Although the authorship of the idea of colonizing Africa may be debatable, we assert unqualifiedly, that to Virginia belongs the honor of making the first efforts in the United States to reduce it to successful practice. And as Virginia took the lead, so she has sustained herself in the van of the enterprise thus far. Perhaps no State in the Union has had more opprobrium cast upon her by abolitionists, foreign and domestic, than Virginia; yet this noble State has held on her course with a steadiness that all her enemies have been unable to disturb.

Mr. Jefferson was among the first that broached the subject. He did it in such a way as to show that his mind was deeply impressed with it; but he recommended no plan, indeed he had not matured a plan satisfactory to himself. When the African colonization scheme was brought forward, Mr. Jefferson gave it his decided approbation.

To Dr. Thornton, a Virginian, belongs the honor of being the first who "seriously contemplated sending a colony to Africa." In the year 1787, before the colonization of Sierra Leone, it will be observed, "Dr. Thornton not only formed a plan of African colonization, but actually attempted its execution, intending to become himself the leader of the colony. He published an 'Address' to the free people of color in Rhode Island and Massachusetts, inviting them to accompany him to the western coast of Africa, with the view of planting a colony in the land of their forefathers." This effort of Dr. Thornton was too much in advance of the times, as were the other efforts. It had not been sufficiently discussed; it had not matured in the public mind, without which nothing of the sort can succeed in this country; it therefore failed. Dr. Thornton lived, however, to see his plan carried out successfully by the Colonization Society, of which he was an officer.

In the year 1800, the Legislature of Virginia, in secret session, "*Resolved,* that the Governor be requested to correspond with the President of the United States on the subject of purchasing lands, without the limits of this State, whither persons obnoxious to the laws, or dangerous to the peace of society, may be removed." Mr. Monroe, then governor of Virginia, opened a correspondence with Mr. Jefferson, then President of the United States. All understood the resolution to refer to persons of color, but its language was so ambiguous, that both Mr. Monroe and Mr. Jefferson doubted of its import. The correspondence which had ensued on the resolution was submitted to the Session of 1802, when the Legislature passed the following resolution: "*Resolved,* That the Governor be requested to correspond with the President of the United States, for the purpose of obtaining a place, without the limits of the same, to which free Negroes, or Mulattoes, and such Negroes or Mulattoes as may be emancipated, may be sent, or choose to remove, as a place of asylum." The Legislature directed the Governor "to prefer the continent of Africa, or any of the Spanish or Portuguese settlements in South America." Here the matter rested until 1804.

Mr. Jefferson, in 1804, revived the correspondence on this subject with Governor Page, in which he expresses a preference for the territory of Louisiana, just purchased by the United States. Governor Page submitted Mr. Jefferson's letter to the Legislature. The Legislature passed a resolution in conformity with Mr. Jefferson's suggestion, in January, 1805. Nothing was accomplished, however, by this resolution.

After this, Ann Mifflin, supposed to belong to the Society of Friends, "had conceived the plan of a colony on the western coast of Africa, and, through a Mr. Lynd, applied to Mr. Jefferson for his opinion respecting the practicability of such an enterprise." Mr. Jefferson returned Mr. Lynd a long and detailed answer, dated in 1811, in which he says: "You have asked my opinion on the proposition of Ann Mifflin, to take measures for procuring, on the coast of Africa, an establishment to which the people of color of these States might from time to time be colonized, under the auspices of different governments. Having long ago made up my mind on this subject, I have no hesitation in saying that I have ever thought that the most desirable measure which could be adopted, for gradually drawing off this part of our population – most advantageous for themselves as well as for us. Going from a country possessing all the useful arts, they might be the means of transplanting them among the inhabitants of Africa, and would thus carry back to the country of their origin the seeds of civilization, which might render their sojournment here a blessing in the end to that country." Mr. Jefferson says further: "I received, in the last year of my entering into the administration of the general government, a letter from the governor of Virginia, consulting me, at the request of the Legislature of the State, on the means of procuring some such asylum, to which these people might be occasionally sent. I proposed to him the establishment of Sierra Leone. I directed Mr. King, American envoy in London, to ascertain whether Negroes from this country would be admitted into the colony. Mr. King wrote: 'That the colony was going on in but a languishing condition; that the funds of the company were likely to fail, as they received no return of profit to keep them up; that they were then in treaty with the government to take the establishment off their hands, but that in no event should they be willing to receive more of these people from the United States, as it was that portion of settlers who had gone from the United States, who, by their idleness and turbulence, had kept the settlement in constant danger of dissolution.'" In this letter, Mr. Jefferson writes: "Nothing is more to be wished than that the United States would themselves undertake to make such an establishment on the coast of Africa." The war with Great Britain coming on shortly after this, nothing more was done until 1816.

Here we see that the public mind in Virginia was, for several years, closely occupied with this subject; her most distinguished statesmen had it under consideration, and alluded to it in their conversations and correspondence. It affords the intelligent mind much pleasure to watch the progress of this great measure, as it passed from its incipiency to its accomplishment.

Section 5

Immediately after the war the discussion of the subject was revived. Gen. Charles Fenton Mercer, a member of the Virginia Legislature, "heard, by mere accident, of the secret resolutions which had been passed at former sessions, and having satisfied himself of their nature, by reference to the recorded minutes of the House, resolved to bring up the subject anew." With regard to the resolutions, Gen. Mercer says: "With respect to the first of them (the secret resolutions), I can truly say, that the intelligence broke in upon me like a ray of light through the profoundest gloom, and by a mere accident which occurred in the spring of 1816; that upon two several occasions, very early in the present century, the General Assembly of Virginia had invited the aid of the United States to obtain a territory, beyond their limits, whereon to colonize certain portions of our colored population. For the evidence of these facts, then new to me, I was referred to the clerk of the Senate, by the friend who revealed them, and in the private records of that body I found them verified."

Upon this information, Gen. Mercer concerted with Francis S. Key, of Georgetown, and Elias B. Caldwell, of Washington City, a plan for carrying the object of the resolutions into execution. Accordingly, in December, 1816 ("prior to the organization of the Colonization Society, but with a view to its approaching formation," of which Gen. Mercer had been informed by Mr. Key), Gen. Mercer introduced into the "House of Delegates, a resolution which stands recorded on its journal, asking the aid of the General Government, to procure in Africa, or elsewhere beyond the limits of the United States, a territory on which to colonize our free people of color, who might be disposed to avail themselves of such an asylum, and such of our slaves as their masters might please to emancipate."

The name of Rev. Robert Finley, D.D., of the borough of Princeton, in the State of New Jersey, must always find a conspicuous place, in speaking of the early efforts of African colonization. Dr. Finley had thought much on the subject of the free persons of color in the United States. In 1815, he wrote a letter to John O. Mumford, Esq., of New York, from which it is manifest that he had the scheme of colonization in Africa fully in his mind, more than a year before Gen. Mercer knew anything about the secret resolutions. No sooner had Dr. Finley matured his plans than he took measures to carry them into practical effect. He embraced every opportunity of proposing the scheme to his friends: "all seemed to admit that the design was good, both as it related to the free Negroes and to the dark continent of Africa; but few of them could be persuaded, however, that there was any probability that such a scheme could be carried into effect; and although they did not oppose it, they did not at once enter very zealously into his views."

Colonization we regard as a providential measure, as it stands connected with the ultimate purpose. Providential arrangements are perfected through instrumentalities. The individuals and bodies engaged in forming the scheme of colonization, were but the instruments Providence employed for the purpose of its accomplishment – this is the first consideration. Another is, that colonization is a Southern measure; concocted by Southern men, and sustained, principally, by Southern means. To show that we are correct in what we here state, we refer to the facts, that when Dr. Finley proposed the plan to Northern men, if they did not shrink from it, they received it but coldly, and no one proposed cooperation, or aid, in any way. Gen. Mercer's applications were to Southern men. No sooner were his propositions submitted, than they awakened in them the determination of putting the plan into immediate operation. Gen. Mercer says: "I repaired to the city of Baltimore, where, by sundry addresses to the people, in one of which I was sustained by Francis S. Key, and by personal applications to the citizens (in which I was accompanied from place to place for many days, by Robert Purviance), we succeeded in obtaining a subscription of near five thousand dollars, to defray the expenses of the expedition of Mess'rs Mills and Burgess, to explore the coast of Africa, in order to select a suitable place for the proposed colony." We submit another view, to show that colonization is a Southern measure – suppose the South should withdraw from it. Who does not see that it would immediately fail? Suppose the North should withdraw from it, would that defeat the measure? Not at all – that would but slightly retard it. But in such an enterprise there is room enough for all, East, West, North and South.

Section 6

The preliminary arrangements having been made, on the 21st of December, 1816, a public meeting was called in the city of Washington, over which Mr. Clay presided. On taking the chair, Mr. Clay made a speech, stating the objects of the meeting to be, to devise the plans necessary to the colonizing, in Africa, the free persons of color in the United States; and of forming an association for the purpose of executing that object. "This class of the mixed population of our country," said Mr. Clay, "was peculiarly situated: they neither enjoyed the immunities of freemen, nor were they subject to the incapacities of slaves, but partook, in some degree, of the qualities of both. From their condition, and the unconquerable prejudices resulting from their color, they never could amalgamate with the free whites of this country. It was desirable, therefore, both as it respected them and the residue of the population of the country, to draw them off. Various schemes of colonization had been thought of, and a part of our continent, it was thought by some, might furnish a suitable establishment for them, but for his part he had a decided preference for some part of the coast of Africa: there, ample provision might be made for the colony itself, and it might be rendered instrumental to the introduction into that extensive quarter of the globe, of the arts, civilization and Christianity."

Mr. Caldwell addressed the meeting, stating the benefits to be derived by the free people of color in the United States, forming a government in Africa, where they and their children might live and enjoy rights and privileges which they could not enjoy here.

Mr. Randolph also addressed the meeting: he said, "that there was nothing in the proposition submitted to consideration, *which in the smallest degree touched another very important and delicate question which ought to be left as much out of view as possible.* But it appeared to him, that it had not been sufficiently insisted on, with a view to obtain the cooperation of all the citizens of the United States, not only that this meeting does not, in any wise, affect the question of negro slavery, but as far as it goes, must materially tend to secure the property of every master in the United States, over his slaves. It was a notorious fact, that the existence of this mixed and intermediate population of free Negroes, was viewed by every slave-holder as one of the greatest sources of the insecurity and unprofitableness of slave property; that they serve to excite in their fellow beings a feeling of discontent, of repining at their situation, and that they act as channels of communication, not only between different slaves, but between the slaves of different districts; that they are the depositaries of stolen goods, and the promoters of mischief. In a worldly point of view then, without entering into the general question, and apart from those higher and nobler motives which had been presented to the meeting, *the owners of slaves were interested in providing a retreat for this part of our population.*

After the speeches had been delivered, Mr. Caldwell offered a preamble and resolutions, which were adopted the third in the series, is, *"Resolved,* That Francis S. Key, Bushrod Washington, Elias B. Caldwell, James Breckinridge, Walter Jones, Richard Rush, and William G. D. Worthington, be a committee to prepare a constitution and rules for the government of the association or society, above mentioned, and report the same to the next meeting for consideration." The meeting then adjourned until the following Saturday, when it again assembled in the Hall of the House of Representatives. At that meeting the committee reported a constitution, which was unanimously adopted.

The first article of the constitution provides, that "This Society shall be called, The American Society for colonizing the free people of color of the United States."

The second article declares the object of the Society: "The object to which its attention is to be exclusively directed, is to promote and execute a plan for colonizing, with their consent, the free people of color residing in our country, in Africa, or such other places as Congress shall deem most expedient. And the Society shall act, to effect this object, in cooperation with the General Government, and such of the States as may adopt regulations upon the subject."

The Society having been formed, it proceeded, on the 1st day of January, 1817, to elect officers; Hon. Bushrod Washington was elected president. The vice-presidents were Hon. William H. Crawford, Hon. Henry Clay, Hon. William Phillips, Col, Henry Rutgers, Hon. John E. Howard, Hon. Samuel Smith, Hon. John C. Herbert, John Taylor, Esq., Gen. Andrew Jackson, Robert Ralston, Esq., Richard Rush, Esq., Gen. John Mason, Rev. Robert Finley.

The Board of Managers were, Francis S. Key, Walter Jones, John Laird, Rev. Dr. James Laurie, Rev. Stephen B. Balch,

Rev. Obadiah B. Brown, James H. Blake, John Peter, Edmund J. Lee, William Thornton, Jacob Hoffman, Henry Carrol.

The sole object of the Society, it will be observed, is, THE COLONIZING, IN AFRICA, THE FREE PEOPLE OF COLOR IN THE UNITED STATES, WITH THEIR CONSENT. This is the only proposition that the Society makes: to this proposition it has faithfully adhered during the whole time of its existence, which now nearly covers the period of four decades of years.

An expounder of the principles of the Society says: "We resort to no formidable, violent measures, in the pursuit of our object. Mild, temperate, moderate, exciting no apprehensions, it appeals to Heaven for the continuation of that countenance and support which it has hitherto deigned to extend to us. This Society has constantly protested, from its origin down to the present time, that we have not, do not, and never will, interfere upon the subject of slavery as it exists in the United States. It is no part of our purpose or office to do that. These are our principles, and with these and perseverance, success, in my opinion, is beyond all human doubt."

The purposes of the Society are shown in another form, to wit: "1. To rescue the free colored people of the United States from their political and social disadvantages. 2. To place them in a country where they may enjoy the benefits of free government, with all the blessings which it brings in its train. 3. To spread civilization, sound morals, and true religion, throughout the continent of Africa. 4. To arrest and destroy the slave-trade. 5. To afford slave-owners, who wish or are willing to liberate their slaves, an asylum for their reception."

The consummate prudence with which the affairs of the Society have been conducted, challenges the admiration of all. It is difficult to imagine how any one could object to a measure so desirable as this Society proposes to accomplish; yet the abolitionists, true to their instincts have made the Society the object of their fiercest opposition and most violent denunciation, from the day of its organization to the present time.

The parent Society holds meetings in Washington City, annually. Auxiliary Societies have been formed in the States of Maine,

Vermont, Massachusetts, Connecticut, New York, New Jersey, Pennsylvania, Delaware, Virginia, North Carolina, Georgia, Alabama, Mississippi, Louisiana, Tennessee, Kentucky, Ohio, Indiana, Illinois, Missouri, and Iowa. Maryland has a separate and independent organization; sending out her own colonists; and, in every way, acting for herself; her colony is Cape Palmas.

Many of the States have passed acts to favor the object of the Society. In 1817, Georgia passed an act, authorizing the Governor to demand and receive "any Negroes, Mulattoes, or persons of color, as may have been, or hereafter may be seized or condemned," under the act of Congress passed in 1807, prohibiting the importation of slaves after the 1st day of January, 1808. The act referred to, authorized the Governor to sell such slaves, or to turn them over to the Colonization Society, upon the Society paying "all expenses incurrred by the State, since they have been captured and condemned. *His Excellency the Governor is authorized and requested to aid in promoting the benevolent views of said Society, in such manner as he may deem expedient.*" According to the provisions of this act, the Governor turned over to the Society thirty-four Africans, who were condemned under the act of 1817; they were by the Society restored to their country. It is, perhaps, proper to remark here, that the General Government, by its agents, attends to the interests of re-captured Africans, and that the thirty-four above alluded to, were of that description.

Section 7

The Society having made the proper arrangements, in 1821, sent out the first company of colonists. And here it should be remarked, "that Congress, on the 3d day of March, 1819, the last day of its session, passed an act authorizing the President of the United States to institute an agency in Africa, for the purpose of providing an asylum for such Africans as should be liberated by our ships-of-war, from vessels seized in violation of the provisions of the law for the suppression of the slave-trade." Rev. Samuel Bacon, a minister of the Protestant Episcopal Church, was appointed agent; he had been previously in the service of the Society. As soon as Mr. Bacon landed in Africa, and cast his eyes over the vast field that it presented, he exclaimed, "What a field for evangelical labor amongst them! How lamentable, that these fine people do not attract the notice of the religious world!" In a letter to a friend in Philadelphia, he says, "You may depend on it, there is work for us here; there is work for missionaries, for teachers, for good men of all descriptions. I am struck with wonder at the native Africans. The sickly and depressed countenance of a Philadelphia colored man, is not to be seen amongst them. A noble aspect, a dignified mien, a frank and open countenance, is the entire demeanor of the wild man."

The whole number of emigrants sent to Liberia by the Society, up to this time (1855), is eight thousand eight hundred and thirty-four; of this number, five thousand and twenty-seven were emancipated by their owners. The Maryland Colonization Society has sent to Africa about twelve hundred emigrants. We are not apprized of the number of free persons, included in the Maryland emigrants, but suppose it to be very small, not exceeding, perhaps, two hundred. The present population of Liberia is estimated at about ten thousand Americans and their children, and upwards of two hundred thousand natives. Many of the latter number were re-captured from slavers by our ships-of-war cruising on the African coast. By the treaty of Washington, commonly called the Ashburton treaty, the principal object of which was the settlement of the northwestern boundary question – a question left open from the period of the war of the Revolution, it was agreed that both England and the United States should keep a naval armament, of not less than eighty guns, constantly on the African coast. By the vessels thus employed many vessels engaged in the slave trade are captured. The slaves from these captured vessels are conveyed to the colony, and turned over to an agent of the government, who looks after their welfare. In addition to the English and American ships-of-war employed on the African coast, the French Government has a force there. Notwithstanding the activity and vigilance of all these ships-of-war, five-sixths of the vessels engaged in the trade escape capture, and land and dispose of their cargoes. The Society, in the accomplishment of its undertaking, has raised much money. From the fact that during the early years of the Society, no distinction was made in the treasurer's accounts, it is impossible to ascertain how much was contributed by the South, and how much by the North; but we have been kindly furnished, by Rev. W. M'Lain, Secretary of the Society, with the following table, which will show the contributions from the Southern States for ten consecutive years:

Receipts of the Am. Col. Society from the Slave-holding States, from 1846 to 1855 inclusive.

States	1846	1847	1848	1849	1850	1851	1852	1853	1854	1855
Maryland	$228.55	$248.62	$13.00	$74.36	$226.98	$40.00	$1,475.29	$2,147.26	$458.16	$2,245.78
Dist. Col.			32.00	489.67	358.92	868.00	377.78	986.83	1,235.28	1,482.14
Virginia	1,194.63	1,571.20	1,473.11	1,552.51	6,248.77	3,080.52	9,500.04	10,192.58	12604.52	2,757.86
No. Car.		12.78	32.00	601.81	1,102.34	1,393.12	713.20	1,354.25	128.75	221.58
So. Car.	115.12	25.00	78.50	49.00	24.00		60.00	10.00	41.00	82.00
Georgia	150.00	142.50	662.35	305.50	5,197.50	885.25	634.00	3,500.25	680.00	512.60
Florida						10.00	20.00		1.00	31.00
Alabama	347.50	5.00	510.00	93.50	369.60	463.95	1,058.57	622.00	710.50	25.00
Miss'ippi	6,012.80	1,000.00	1,228.50	592.00	1,866.50	2,527.62	3,304.50	6,675.25	2,195.25	1,073.87
Louisiana	729.25	176.78		7.00	392.00	2,657.70	3,426.65	1,314.21	794.00	812.96
Texas							2.50		5.00	16.00
Tennessee	316.00	268.50	69.30	672.67	4,070.12	1,440.50	1,526.85	2,664.66	1,558.50	570.00
Kentucky	3,454.98	3,470.00	2,594.50	1,728.23	1,578.23	1,997.60	697.36	4,060.50	2,916.80	2,833.00
Missouri	107.50		142.00	8.18	205.00	110.00	622.58	120.00	965.85	133.00
Arkansas		17.00		5.00	117.50	45.00	633.60			516.00

AGGREGATE AMOUNTS FOR THE TEN YEARS

Maryland	$6,680.83	Florida	$62.00
Dist. Col.	6,307.74	Alabama	4,205.62
Virginia	50,176.70	Mississippi	26,476.29
North Carolina	5,559.83	Louisiana	10,310.55
South Carolina	484.62	Texas	23.50
Georgia	12,669.90	Tennessee	13,157.10
		Kentucky	$25,331.20
		Missouri	2,414.11
		Arkansas	1,394.10
		Total	165,454.09

Total aggregate receipts from all the States $480,795.49

Section 8

The last United States census shows that there are in the Southern States two hundred and thirty-six thousand free persons of color. Whence came they? The answer is, they were emancipated by their owners. Estimating the average value of these emancipated slaves to be five hundred dollars each, we have the aggregate sum of one hundred and eighteen millions of dollars.

Free Negroes, as everybody except the abolitionist knows, are very objectionable amongst the slave population; much of the mischief committed may be traced to them as its source. Besides, the liberty possessed by emancipated slaves here, is of no real benefit to them, but rather a disadvantage; therefore, the legislatures of the respective States, in order to prevent the increase of their numbers, have been compelled to pass laws forbidding their emancipation.

Has the South stopped at the bare emancipation of these slaves? Not at all. As soon as it was fully understood that the freed slave realized no benefit from his new condition, means for the promotion of his well-being have been devised; for the truth of this remark we point to the Colonization Society. That organization is exclusively for the benefit of free persons of color. In Africa they may enjoy a real freedom; a freedom that is only nominal here.

By the table exhibited in the preceding section, it will be perceived that the aggregate sum received from the North and the South, is four hundred and eighty thousand, seven hundred and ninety-five dollars and forty-nine cents. Of this sum, the South contributed one hundred and sixty-five thousand, four hundred and fifty-four dollars and nine cents; leaving to the North the sum of three hundred and fifteen thousand, three hundred and forty-one dollars and forty cents. At the first view, it would appear that the North has contributed much more than the South, but this supposition is removed by the fact, that the contributions of the South have been made in money *and property*. We cannot state precisely the amount of property contributed by the South, but we may safely say, that six thousand slaves have been by their owners turned over to the Colonization Society. If these slaves be put down at their average value of five hundred dollars each, their aggregate value would be three millions dollars; to this add the sum of one hundred and sixty-five thousand, four hundred and fifty-four dollars and nine cents, contributed in money, and we have the sum of three millions, one hundred and sixty-five thousand four hundred and fifty-four dollars and nine cents, as the amount directly advanced by the South in African Colonization.

But, in order that we may see, in one view, the offerings of the South, direct and incidental, *in the great enterprise of African emancipation,* to the above sum of three millions, one hundred and sixty-five thousand, four hundred and fifty-four dollars and nine cents, we must add the sum of one hundred and eighteen millions of dollars, as the value of the free persons of color now in the Southern States: then, we have the grand total of *one hundred and twenty-one millions, one hundred and sixty-five thousand, four hundred and fifty-four dollars and nine cents,* as the contribution of the South! The world's history does not furnish another instance of such munificent and disinterested benevolence.

But we need pursue this subject no farther; for whatever else may be said of the operations of the African Colonization Society, passes more properly into the history of Liberia: we conclude, therefore, by remarking, that there has never been an enterprise undertaken by Americans, that united in its support more, or as many, men of distinguished character, in all the walks of life, than the enterprise of African Colonization. Amongst the most conspicuous of its friends, now numbered with the dead, are Jefferson, Madison, Monroe, Jackson, Crawford, Clay, Randolph, Washington and Marshall; names which shall continue to gather fresh lustre, as they move down the stream of time, to the last.

One word more and our task will be finished. While the good, the wise, the patriotic, have been engaged in building up a government, in whose destiny is involved countless millions of our race, what have the abolitionists been about? The answer is both brief and simple – *brooding mischief and stealing Negroes.*

Made in the USA
Columbia, SC
23 October 2020